'The crucifixion of our Lord is the sternest rebuke to man's selfishness this world has ever seen. Every human life hangs in the balance of this one pivotal event. I encourage you to read this wonderful book by Martin Robinson which portrays the cross as the centrepiece of human history.' – *Dr Neil T. Anderson, President, Freedom in Christ Ministries*

'A model of clarity and control, providing insight and direction through one of the most complex areas of Christian theology. This "survey of the wondrous cross" brings light to the darkness, understanding to our adoration and brings out the contemporary signif-icance of God's act of redemption.' – *David Spriggs, Project Director, The Open Book*

'An excellent primer on the cross.' – *Colin Dye, Senior Pastor at Kensington Temple*

The Rev. Dr Martin Robinson is a Director of the Bible Society, a minister in the Churches of Christ, and author of a number of distinguished books including *Planting Tomorrow's Churches Today* and *The Faith of the Unbeliever.*

THE *THINKING CLEARLY* SERIES

Series editor: Clive Calver

The *Thinking Clearly* series sets out the main issues in a variety of important subjects. Written from a mainstream Christian standpoint, the series combines clear biblical teaching with up-to-date scholarship. Each of the contributors is an authority in his or her field. The series is written in straightforward everyday language, and each volume includes a range of practical applications and guidance for further reading.

The series has two main aims:
1. To help Christians understand their faith better.
2. To show how Christian truths can illuminate matters of crucial importance in our society.

THE *THINKING CLEARLY* SERIES

Series editor: Clive Calver

Why the Cross?

MARTIN ROBINSON

MONARCH
BOOKS

Mill Hill, London NW7 3SA and Grand Rapids, Michigan

First published by Monarch Books in the UK in 2000,
Concorde House, Grenville Place,
Mill Hill, London, NW7 3SA.

Published in the USA by Monarch Books 2001.

Distributed by:
UK: STL, PO Box 300, Kingstown Broadway, Carlisle,
Cumbria CA3 0QS;
USA: Kregel Publications, PO Box 2607
Grand Rapids, Michigan 49501.

ISBN 1 85424 337 3 (UK)
ISBN 0 8254 6021 2 (USA)

British Library Cataloguing Data
A catalogue record for this book is available
from the British Library.

Book design and production for the publishers by
Bookprint Creative Services,
P.O. Box 827, BN21 3YJ, England.
Printed in Great Britain.

Contents

Preface   9

1. The Paradox of the Cross   13

2. Telling the Story   33

3. The Cross and the Mission of Paul   51

4. A Sacrificial Death   69

5. The Reconciling Cross   85

6. It is for Freedom that Christ has Set Us Free   103

7. Evil and the God of Love   121

8. The Cross and our Present Cry   139

Preface

When I was asked to write a book on the cross for the 'Thinking Clearly' series my first reaction was one of great excitement. My motivation flowed from an awareness that few Christians could speak with much coherence as to what the death of Jesus had to do with them. If this is true for Christians it is even more so for those who stand outside the Church. For some Christians it is clear that Jesus had to die in order to be raised and that his confrontation with the powers of his day made that death rather likely. Others are aware that the death of Jesus somehow relates to forgiveness but often this is merely expressed in slogans frequently seen on church notice boards – 'Jesus Christ died for our sins' – but talking intelligently about what such slogans mean usually proves much more difficult.

It does not follow that Christians regard the cross as unimportant or incidental to their understanding or experience of the Christian faith, only that it is hard to understand and even harder to express. The invitation to explore this area was therefore a privilege. However, my second reaction was to be daunted by the large number of books already written on the subject, some of which must be regarded as classics.

Why then write another book on the subject? An overview

of the literature reveals that it tends to fall into two categories. The one category is that of theological reflection of a fairly robust and sometimes impenetrable nature. These books are inaccessible for the ordinary reader. The other category is that of popular devotion with little theological reflection. This book is an attempt to write at a popular level while at the same time moving beyond a devotional to a reflective style that does attempt to deal with theological themes in an accessible manner. The reader can judge to what extent the book succeeds in this attempt. There are some other books which probably mirror this attempt, not least of which is John Stott's book on the cross. I have attempted to keep his book in mind while approaching the task in a different kind of way.

The process of writing the book soon revealed a further difficulty. The cross is so central to the Christian faith that any book on this subject all too easily becomes a book on every aspect of the Christian faith. The questions of evil and of suffering, of the incarnation, of the nature of Christ's person, of salvation, of the doctrine of the last things, and of the resurrection are just a few of the more obvious questions that are so intimately related to the cross that it is hard to draw boundaries. I have attempted to keep as close as possible to an actual consideration of the meaning of the cross itself and avoid being drawn into a discussion of related topics.

All authors are encouraged to have in mind a particular audience for the book that they are writing. I have attempted to write in the first place for Christians who want to think around the subject of the cross and to do so in such a way that the book could be given to those who are not Christians but who might have raised questions about the meaning of the Christian faith. In particular it could be an aid for those who have recently attended one or other of the various groups designed to explore the

Christian faith but who have more questions that can be adequately answered in a group session. Some of the chapters might lend themselves to group discussion and I have actually used some of the early drafts of the book in a home group setting.

It has only been possible for me to overcome the problem of surveying the wide range of literature because of the invaluable help offered by my researcher Linsi Simmonds. I am immensely grateful to her for all the thoughtful suggestions she has made in the writing of this work.

While every author wants their readers to enjoy reading the book that they have written, the subject of the cross does not really produce a book that someone picks up for light entertainment. If enjoyment does not easily flow from these pages then I hope that a degree of wonder and amazement will. The late Cardinal Hume, writing about the cross, quotes an Orthodox theologian in this way:

'We see that it is not the task of Christianity to provide easy answers to every question, but to make us progressively aware of a mystery. God is not so much the object of our knowledge as the cause of our wonder.' (1)

Notes

1. Basil Hume, *The Mystery of the Cross*, p.5.

1

The Paradox of the Cross

The opening chapter examines the impact of the cross on the early Christian community. It points to the fact that the death of Jesus raised a number of very important questions for his followers. Their first response was to attempt to find answers in the pages of the Old Testament and the key passages used by the early Church are explored in terms of the meaning that the first Christians gave to them.

The Paradox of the Cross

Almost two decades ago, I worked as a minister in a small and sometimes struggling, inner-city congregation. It was not just the church that struggled in that environment. It was tough to live among decrepit high-rise tower blocks, interspersed with damp maisonettes and heavily vandalised local shopping centres. Even the local packs of dogs tended to look somewhat despairing as they searched in vain for morsels of food in the upturned rubbish bins. Hope was a commodity in short supply.

From the windows of many of the high-rise flats it was possible to see the skyline of the city centre and in particular to see a large illuminated cross fixed on the tower of a church in the city. It wasn't a particularly beautiful cross and in the daytime it looked entirely uninspiring but at night it shone brightly and visibly for miles. I couldn't help being struck by the number of people who lived in those flats who told me that often at night, sometimes when they felt particularly low, they would gaze at that lighted cross and draw comfort and encouragement. 'Perhaps God does

15

still care for me,' was the sentiment they expressed. Hope welled up in the midst of heartache and difficulty.

At about the same time as I listened to these expressions of gratitude for a simple lit cross, I was visiting a city in the Far East. The occasion was a conference of Christian leaders, and one of the leaders from a predominantly Muslim context told me of a very different view of the cross. A church near where he lived had applied to the authorities for permission to expand their building. They had been given permission on the condition that no cross appear on the extended building and that they took down the very large cross on the building they already had. The church decided not to extend on those terms.

The cross has often aroused very different and sometimes extreme emotions. Hope, joy, gratitude, wonder, confidence and even amazement on the one hand; anger, offence, scandal and controversy on the other. At first sight this range of emotions might seem puzzling. Why should the cross have come to assume such a central role in the life of the Christian community and why should others find it so offensive? Why should such a simple symbol arouse such passions? The clue to understanding this variety of emotions lies in the word 'symbol'. It is obviously not the cross as a physical construct that is so offensive – it is the recognition, whether conscious or not, of what it stands for, of what lies behind it.

The actual origins of the use of this symbol are worth some reflection. A marketing man who is also a Christian and a good friend, caught my attention once by describing the symbol of the cross as a marketing man's dream. I wanted to know what he meant by that. He responded by saying, 'It meets all the criteria for a marketing icon – it's simple in its construction, it can be endlessly reworked in a variety of settings, it can be reproduced even by a child, it is easy to remember and everyone associates it with the product. At that level it rivals the famous Mercedes three-pointed star.'

But it was not a marketing consultant that first suggested using the symbol of the cross as the primary Christian symbol. Nor was it the early Church or even the early Church fathers that did so. Widespread use of the symbol only took place after Constantine's vision of a cross acted as a prophetic inspiration for him on the eve of a particularly important battle.

The church historian J.W.C. Wand tells us:

> In 312 he (Constantine) was met and crushed at the Milvian Bridge. The battle marks an epoch, for it helped to make the first Christian Emperor and so affected the history of European civilisation down to the present time. It was during the night before this battle that Constantine is generally believed to have seen the cross of light in the sky with the words *In hoc sigmo vinces*. Hence came the *Labarum*, the famous standard of Constantine, a spearhead forming the cross with the *Chi Rho*, the initial Greek letters of the name of Christ, enclosed in a circle.[1]

They would fight under the protection of the cross. Constantine's subsequent victory and the tabloid attraction of the story was enough to cause the symbol of the cross to become the universal, widespread symbol of Christians. The predominant use of the cross supplanted the earlier use of symbols as diverse as the fish, the peacock and the dove. Today, the cross has taken such a central place as a Christian symbol that few Christian buildings would not contain some reference to a cross somewhere.

But the original widespread usage of the cross as a symbol was not just related to the sponsorship of Constantine. Influential and important as he was, the cross as a centre of devotional and doctrinal concern had already assumed a place of importance in the total life of the Christian community. Admittedly it had taken a number of years for this to happen, but slowly, inevitably, this terrible sign of appalling cruelty, this instrument of torture and means of execution acted as a focus for reflection for the emerging Christian church.

Even before the actual process of thinking clearly about the cross began, the events of the cross and the subsequent resurrection formed a central part of the Christian story. 'This Jesus whom you crucified' was a consistent part of the teaching of the apostles who recounted the events of the Christian story long before the Church had fully thought through the meaning of the story. The recounting of these gospel events necessarily provoked a process of reflection as to their meaning.

In one sense, Jesus began the process of reflection while still on the cross. The words quoted by the Gospel writer, 'My God, my God, why have you forsaken me?' were ambiguous and needed interpretation. Was Jesus finally giving up on his sense of call? Did he feel that it was all over, that his total ministry had failed? Or was this actually a conscious quotation of the Messianic lines from Psalm 21? However one understands these particular words of Jesus, the question of how to understand the death of Jesus inevitably formed in the mind of his disciples from the moment that his death and burial was completed.

The disciples' initial and possibly despairing reflection was transformed by their encounter with the risen Christ. In the light of this unexpected and unparalleled event, the apparent tragedy of the cross was revisited by the disciples. The question now was not the earlier one – has the death of Jesus ended everything? A stream of questions now flowed. Why did Jesus have to die? Was the death of Jesus failure or fulfilment? If it was fulfilment then how did that operate? Couldn't God have accomplished his purpose without the shock and suffering of the death and resurrection of Jesus? If not, then what did it all signify? What is the core meaning of the death and resurrection of Jesus?

The various 'meaning' type questions related to the actual events of the cross soon spread further. It does not require much imagination to see how these central events provoked two further kinds of questioning. The first kind related to the person of Jesus himself. Who was this man? The first easy answer of the disciples prior to the cross was to identify Jesus as the Messiah. But the death and resurrection of Jesus suggested that their original notions of Messiahship needed some revision. If he was a man then he was no ordinary man. If he was not an ordinary man then who precisely was he?

The second set of questions linked issues about the cross itself and the person of Jesus to wider matters of meaning. If the cross was linked in some way to salvation, to reconciliation with God, then how did that translate into the really big questions. What is the purpose of our lives? How is evil dealt with? How can we live so that the kingdom that Jesus spoke of might come? What does the cross say about the community that has now formed to live out the story? How does the cross foreshadow the end times?

There is virtually no issue in the whole of Christian thinking that is not related in some way to that of the cross and the events that surrounded it. In particular, the cross raises the question as to who it was that was crucified. If it was the Messiah, or the Son of God that was executed then questions must be asked about his birth. The death of the Son of God prompts reflection on the ultimate victory of God over evil. It causes questions to be asked about the nature of the kingdom that Jesus came to proclaim. The questions continue to multiply. In a very real sense, the action of Constantine in claiming the public protection of the cross only brought to a specific public reality that which was already present in the minds of Christians. The cross is and was central to the Christian message, to the way in which Christians are called to live and to the core devotional and worship life of the Christian community. In seizing hold of the cross, Constantine had a very receptive audience.

Beginning at the beginning

If it is true that the death of Jesus provoked large numbers of significant questions for the early Christian community, how can we begin to understand the event, significance and relevance of this key moment for the Christian faith? In particular how can we come to grips with this central question – why should it matter that one single man died at the hands of an executioner in distant Palestine, all those years ago? Even though the cross and resurrection had a clear formative impact on the origins of Christianity, what has this to do with us? Does the cross still matter to twenty-first-century people? How can it be that the death of one man can have more impact on the whole of humanity than the death of any other? To begin to answer these questions it is necessary to begin where the first Christians had to begin. The documents that make up the New Testament reveal the thinking of the early Christian community in terms of the meaning of the cross and in later chapters we will reflect on what we can learn from this written record. But the first Christians did not begin with the pages of the New Testament. Rather, they turned to the only written document they had of God's dealings with Israel, the Old Testament, in order to understand the meaning of the events that they had witnessed.

The record in the Acts of the Apostles suggests that the resurrected Jesus helped the disciples to interpret all that had happened (Acts 1:1–11). Luke does not tell us explicitly whether these encounters included reference to particular passages in the Old Testament. Although we could speculate on the content of the conversations that the disciples had with their risen Lord, we cannot be certain of what they learnt during these times. What we can know is that a number of Old Testament texts became crucial for the early Christian community in terms of explaining the significance of all that had happened, and in particular in coming to terms with the death of Jesus on the cross. Matthew, more than any of the Gospel writers, looks to the Old Testament as containing prophecies that were fulfilled by the life of Jesus. Luke, in the Acts of the Apostles, shows Peter using the same kind of appeal to the Old Testament in explaining the meaning of the day of Pentecost. The New Testament is notable for its constant allusion to the Old Testament record. Amid this activity, five Old Testament texts stand out as particularly significant in relation to the event of the crucifixion itself.

Isaiah 53

The Isaiah passage which refers to a suffering servant comprises the majority of chapter 53 and is the most

obvious text in the whole of the Old Testament for
Christians to seize upon. This is true for two reasons.
First, Mark suggests that Jesus himself referred to the
passage as a means of understanding his own ministry
and future and that to some degree its contents acted to
guide and nourish him (Mark 14:21).

Second, the astonishing degree of correspondence
between the details of the passage and the death of Jesus
are almost startling. The servant is pierced and wounded.
He was taken away by oppression and judgement and led
like a lamb to the slaughter. His grave was to be with the
wicked (the thieves at either side) and with the rich (the
tomb of Joseph of Arimathea). He didn't open his mouth
(to defend himself) but in his silence was condemned. After
the suffering of his soul he will see the light of life and be
satisfied, which was taken as a reference to the resurrection.

Inevitably the correspondence of the details led the
disciples to use the same passage of Scripture to interpret
its meaning. Three points in particular struck home. First,
this was not a failure of the ministry of Jesus but part of
the purpose of God. He was rejected by men and women,
even humiliated by them and that while this could be
interpreted as signifying the rejection of God, far from
this being the case, it was God's will that he should suffer,
not because God is vindictive but because he had a greater
purpose for his servant.

Second, his death was intimately associated with the
reality of sin. He was wounded for our transgressions. His
punishment brings peace and healing to humankind. The
wrongdoing or iniquity that is part of the life of humanity
was borne by the suffering servant. He bore the sin of many.
His bearing of the burden of sin and his intercession for
transgressors implies the forgiveness of sins.

Third, the action of the suffering servant is not only related to some kind of elaborate and awful sin offering but points to a vital future role. He will be given a place of importance. There is a reward which attaches to the role.

The totality of these lessons suggested that what happened on the cross had a cosmic significance. This was not a promising ministry that was simply derailed and came to a tragic end. The actual end on the cross was always the intended end. The death of Jesus was directly related to dealing with the imperfections of the world brought about by the presence of sin. The death and resurrection of Jesus was not something that related just to these disciples or even to a single generation. This was a drama that had significance for all precisely because it was the wrongdoing or iniquity of all that was involved in the event itself.

Psalm 22

The impact of Psalm 22 upon the followers of Jesus was very similar in character to that of Isaiah 53, and the two passages may very well have been read side by side. Both seemed to describe the actual events of the crucifixion and Jesus directly quotes both passages. In the case of Psalm 22, the dying words of Jesus seemed to his followers to point directly to the first few words of the psalm and so invited their attention to be drawn to the remaining words of the passage. The mocking and insulting behaviour of onlookers is detailed. Perhaps most dramatically of all, the actual accusation contained in the Gospels is found in the psalm (verse 8):

> He trusts in the Lord;
> let the Lord rescue him.

> Let him deliver him,
> Since he delights in him.

Other details include a reference to the physical condition of someone in tremendous pain: 'I am poured out like water, and all my bones are out of joint. My heart has turned to wax; it has melted away within me. My strength is dried up like a potsherd, and my tongue sticks to the roof of my mouth' (Psalm 22:14–15). The circumstances of the casting of lots over his divided clothes is another obvious detail that is contained in the psalm.

As with Isaiah 53 the striking prophetic fulfilment of the passage encouraged the disciples to look to the psalm as a whole for an account of the meaning of the event. Two elements flow from this kind of examination. The first is the recognition that once again the suffering of Jesus was not just an unfortunate tragedy. His suffering had meaning. The very fact that it was predicted in prophecy indicated to the disciples that the purposes of God were somehow being worked out.

Second the reality of suffering so vividly portrayed in the first half of the psalm gives way to triumph and victory in the second part. The nature of that victory is suggested in the middle part of verse 29: 'all who go down to the dust will kneel before him'. There is an eternal reality that flows from the death of Jesus. As a consequence of this event, the rule of God is going to be restored and the one who suffered will be part of this astonishing restoration. The psalm is not clear about how this is going to happen or when it will happen, only that it will take place. 'They will proclaim his righteousness to a people yet unborn – for he has done it' (Psalm 22:31).

Psalm 69

Although Psalm 69 is not nearly as obvious in its application to the death of Jesus as the previous two passages, once the pattern of looking for Old Testament prophecies was established, this psalm was an obvious candidate for consideration. In very general terms it is a psalm that speaks of the extreme suffering of the servant of God. In all probability the psalm directly refers to the trauma of David. Large parts of the psalm can certainly be appropriated by anyone who is undergoing times of hardship or even persecution. But contained within these general themes there seems to be contained at least one very specific verse which for the early Christians could be seen as directly referring to the cross of Jesus.

In verse 21 we read: 'They put gall in my food and gave me vinegar for my thirst.' In addition to this seemingly direct reference to the events surrounding the cross, the early Christians may well have seen a connection between the salvation of God, referred to in verse 29, and activities which please God more than the redemptive act of sacrificing an ox or a bull, mentioned in verses 30 and 31.

Without the impact of Psalm 22 and Isaiah, this seemingly slight connection in Psalm 69 might not have been noticed, but the impact of the other two passages tended to give weight to more slender references elsewhere. All the more so in the case of Psalm 69 because there seems to be encouragement for those who would follow Jesus. The purpose of God in Jesus is tied to the saving of Israel and to the specific inheritance due to 'the children of his servants' – namely, the Christian community. 'Those who love his name will dwell there' (Psalm 69:34–36). In the midst of persecution these were precious promises.

Zechariah 9–14

The few chapters of Zechariah from 9–14 are quoted more often in the passion accounts of the Gospels than any other Old Testament prophetic text. That single fact suggests that they contain great promise for helping the followers of Jesus to understand his death. Chapter 12:10b records, 'They will look on me, the one they have pierced, and they will mourn for him as one mourns for an only child, and grieve bitterly for him as one grieves for a firstborn son.' The one who is pierced is referred to as a shepherd and once again the words of Jesus in his self-description as the 'good shepherd' must have been quickly remembered.

The overall tenor of this part of Zechariah is to encourage believers to look with hope to the future despite the difficulties of the present. There are some specific verses which the disciples would easily link to the events of the cross. For example, Zechariah 11:12 records, 'I told them, "If you think it best, give me my pay; but if not, keep it." So they paid me thirty pieces of silver.' The obvious connection with the payment of Judas would inevitably cause believers to look closely at these verses even apart from any reference to the shepherd.

The vivid imagery of the end time would certainly have fascinated an emerging church, many of whose members did indeed believe that the end of all things was near. Many of the themes found in Zechariah are reworked by the author of the book of Revelation, indicating that these passages had made some impact on the imagination of the early Christian community. More importantly, the identification of Jesus as the shepherd spoken of prophetically in these passages in Zechariah raises deeper questions about the identity of Jesus. Chapter 11 identifies God himself as the shepherd and notes that a time was coming when he as God would be rejected by many of the people. Later, in chapter 13, the shepherd is described as the man who is close to God. Clearly, for the disciples, the shepherd close to God was Jesus, but what did that mean for Jesus' actual identity and relationship with God? The Zechariah passages tend to force the debate.

Leviticus 16

The writer to the Hebrews draws extensively on Leviticus 16 as a way of reflecting on the questions of the identity of Jesus and the reason for his crucifixion. For the author of Hebrews, the Day of Atonement represents a prophetic enactment of the final day of atonement represented by the death of Jesus. The Christ therefore becomes both the high priest and the sacrifice itself. The author makes many typological connections between what he reads in Leviticus and what he writes to the Christian community. The tearing of the veil recorded in Matthew symbolises the tearing of the flesh of Christ. Now all believers have the right to enter into the presence of God (Hebrews 10:19ff).

Under the New Covenant the theological situation has completely changed. There is no longer any need for a Day of Atonement each year. The first Good Friday was the definitive Day of Atonement when man's sins were purged once and for all. Now every man and woman who is in Christ has the right, once reserved only for the high priest, to enter into the presence of God. He could go in but once a year; we can draw near at any time.

Unlike the early Jewish followers of Jesus, Christians no longer celebrate the Day of Atonement. But this does not mean that we can't learn something from it. That is the argument presented by the writer to the Hebrews. He takes a good deal of effort to demonstrate how the action of Christ on the cross was superior to the actions of Aaron with whom Christ is compared. In doing so the writer is trying to anticipate questions that devout Jews might raise. Although they are hardly likely to be our questions, it is worth reflecting on the issues that our forebears felt they needed to consider. Four contrasts are made:

- Unlike Christ, Aaron was a sinner and he therefore needed to offer sacrifice for himself before making atonement for the people. Because Christ is pure and sinless he does not need to make sacrifices for himself (Hebrews 7:26ff).
- Unlike Aaron who had to repeat the sacrifices regularly, Jesus had no need to make anything other than a single sacrifice which stands for all time. The death of Jesus is not an event that will ever be repeated but stands for all eternity (Hebrews 9:6–14, 25ff).
- The rituals performed by Aaron permitted him entry into the earthly sanctuary – the holiest of holies in the temple – the place on earth where God dwelt; Christ's death on a cross brought him into the presence of God in heaven (Hebrews 9:24).
- The need for a constant repetition of Aaron's sacrifices suggested that these sacrifices were incomplete, possibly a sign of that which was to come. By contrast, Christ's once-for-all sacrifice means that we are freed from the burden of sin, assured of complete forgiveness (Hebrews 10:1–18).

Hebrews is a difficult book for many to read and understand. In large measure this is because the audience was one which was thoroughly familiar with the notion of Israel's covenant relationship with God. The intended readers were Jews and the author of Hebrews is trying to answer a question that is implied but never clearly stated. In essence the question was this: What was wrong with the covenant that Israel had with God and how has the death of Jesus put this right?

The questions posed by those who have never experienced the covenant that God had with Israel are inevitably different but just as important. The claim of the early Christian community was that the life, death and resurrection of Jesus effectively ended the old covenant and ushered in a new covenant, one that had been prophesied in the Old Testament, as a covenant written on the hearts of humanity rather than on tablets of stone. Those who have experienced the new covenant naturally want to know how Christ's death relates to the new covenant and what this says about the identity of Jesus himself. The New Testament claim is that Christ's death is not just an unfortunate by-product of the new covenant but is foundational and central. How and why is this so?

The covenants of God

Before tackling these central questions in the succeeding chapters, it is important to give some indication of what 'covenant' actually meant. The word 'testament' can also be translated as covenant. From one perspective we do not just have an Old and New Testament, we have an Old and New Covenant. The Bible is first and foremost an account or record of these two covenants.

Strictly speaking the Old Covenant is actually a suc-
cession of covenants made between God and the repre-
sentatives of Israel. In the culture of Israel and its
neighbours, a covenant was a solemn binding agreement
made between two parties, usually of unequal power.
Inevitably the inequality of relationship meant that one
party was in a position to impose an agreement and the
weaker party was obliged to accept the agreement.
However, it was in the nature of covenants that there
was usually an element of generosity so that the weaker
party actually benefited from the agreement even though it
was a stronger party that determined the terms of the
covenant. There were at least four important covenants
recorded in the Old Testament. The first was the covenant that God made with Noah. Never again would God
flood the earth and destroy humankind. In this agreement,
humankind was the beneficiary of the promise of God and
no terms were imposed on the peoples of the earth. This
was simply an undertaking freely given by God with no
thought of exacting any particular response. Although, of
course, it does not take long to see that to require a
response implies a closer relationship than if no response
is sought.

The second covenant was that made between God and
Abraham. God promised Abraham many descendants
and a particular land in which those descendants could
live. Abraham was required to have faith in God and to
obey God in faith.

The third covenant was the more familiar agreement
inscribed on literal tablets of stone – the covenant between
God and the people of Israel as represented by Moses.
The promise of God was for a land in which to live and for
blessing as a people. The land would be flowing with 'milk

and honey'. They would be protected from their enemies just as they had been freed from captivity in Egypt. In return they were to keep the commandments.

The fourth covenant was also with Israel but this time through God's covenant with David, the second king of Israel. The requirements imposed on Israel were essentially no different to those expressed in the covenant with Moses. It was simply that the context of a settled people and state had changed. This covenant was more like a renewal and affirmation of the previous covenant. It was not a completely new agreement.

All four of these covenants represented focal points around which the character of God is gradually revealed to the people of Israel. At the same time the inability of the people of Israel to honour or keep the covenant promises becomes abundantly clear. Gradually the need for a new covenant relationship, one that is written on the hearts of those who willingly love God, is revealed and foreseen by the prophets, especially by Jeremiah.

The final covenant is therefore the new covenant which the ministry of Jesus ushers in. But this new agreement of the heart is different in many respects. Jesus, the bearer of the new covenant is not just the messenger, as Moses was, nor merely the representative, as David was. According to the writers of the New Testament or Covenant, Jesus was also the one who made the new covenant possible, who formed it and founded it. The death of Jesus was the crucial instrument in all this. How and why this is so we must now explore.

Questions

1. What feelings or reactions come to you when you see the cross as an image?

2. Read Isaiah chapter 53 and note the similarities between the passage and what you know of the death of Jesus. How do you view these similarities, are they mere co-incidence, was the story of the death of Jesus influenced by this passage, or is it more than this?
3. Why do you think the cross as an image is so widely used by Christians today?
4. What covenant do you think God has made with Christians as a result of the cross?
5. What does the death of Jesus tell us about who he was?

Notes

1. J.W.C. Wand, *A History of the Early Church to AD 500*, Methuen & Co Ltd, London, 1974, p.127.

2

Telling the Story

This chapter surveys the way in which each of the Gospel writers presents the story of the cross. It concentrates on the particular meaning of the cross that is contained in each presentation. Finally it deals with the key notion of ransom, dying on behalf of others, that underlies each account.

Telling the Story

During the last two years of my school career, one of the set Shakespeare texts was *Othello*. As part of the course, the class went to see the Royal National Theatre's production, recorded on film and featuring Laurence Olivier as Othello. It was a stunning experience, so much so that I wondered if I might have the emotional energy to watch the play a second time. In the second year of the course we did see the play again. It was in a different theatre, with a different cast and with Othello played by an American actor best known for his parts in cowboy films. This turned out to be considerably less than a stunning experience. In fact it was hugely disappointing, a great anti-climax, but nevertheless, from the point of view of teaching English, an object lesson for all that.

Since those two experiences I have seen *Othello* a number of times in various productions. It has never ceased to amaze me how the same text can be presented in such different ways to convey a range of emotions, evoking a variety of responses in the audiences. More particularly it is surprising how the same text can convey different meanings depending on the interpretation given by producer and actors to the identical lines offered them by the playwright.

The authors of the four Gospels were each working with the same core events in the life of Jesus but the way in which they presented those events suggests a particular interpretation or explanation of the story they told. As I have already indicated in the previous chapter, the writers of the New Testament partly drew on the resources of the Old Testament in helping to understand the story they were telling.

None of the Gospel writers acted alone as an original novelist might. Each was telling the story partly as it was told and understood in the Christian community of which they were members. The audience was that same, growing community. Each of the Gospel writers were members of local Christian communities in different parts of the Roman Empire. Their local traditions are partly reflected in the various presentations of the same central story. Detecting the themes presented in the Gospels helps us to know how the early Christian communities were coming to understand the drama of the cross.

Before we look at each writer in turn, it is important to remind ourselves of an obvious but often forgotten fact. Namely, the last week of the earthly life of Jesus is given a hugely disproportionate amount of space in all four Gospels as compared with the life of Jesus as a whole, or even as compared with the three year period of his ministry. This is so because each writer sees it as the most important week of the life of Jesus, the period that his whole ministry pointed to, the particular events that gave meaning and purpose to his coming and his teaching. All of the incidents of the last week of his ministry point to one single and unprecedented fact – his death upon a cross and his resurrection three days later.

In one sense, each Gospel could be described as a prologue leading to the event of the crucifixion. In another sense, all four Gospels could be seen as a series of stories each of which contribute to our understanding of the final moments of death and resurrection. In other words, the cross is foreshadowed and so illuminated throughout every chapter of every Gospel and not just in the passion narratives themselves. The Gospel writers were not just presenting a drama in as colourful a fashion as possible, nor were they merely offering a series of facts for our interest alone; they wanted to say something about what these same events actually meant.

Mark – The drama of the cross

Although Mark is obviously not the first Gospel in the New Testament order, most scholars agree that Mark was certainly written before Matthew and Luke and that both Matthew and Luke were familiar with Mark when they wrote their Gospels. Therefore it is important to give some consideration to Mark's account before examining the different or in some cases additional meaning found in Matthew and Luke.

It is perhaps not surprising that Luke and Matthew followed Mark to the extent that they did in the composition of their Gospels. One scholar notes that: 'Mark can be divided into 105 sections. Of these sections 93 occur in Matthew and 81 in Luke. Of Mark's 105 sections there are only 4 which do not occur either in Matthew or in Luke.'[1] The essentially dramatic presentation of Mark is echoed in both Matthew and Luke but Mark contains some particular themes that add to the quality of the drama that he presents.

The humanity of Jesus

Mark's picture of Jesus is of a man who makes himself vulnerable. The graphic presentation by Mark of the emotional response of Jesus to a whole range of situations is so stark that both Matthew and Luke tend to soften this aspect of his personality. Jesus could be tired and need to rest (Mark 6:31), he was moved with compassion (Mark 6:34), he marvelled at their unbelief (Mark 6:6), he loved the rich young ruler (Mark 10:21), he could feel hunger (Mark 11:12). The power of Jesus does not lie in the fact that he was an exceptional human being devoid of the normal human responses. He clearly displayed the same kind of emotions that the readers of Mark might also have felt.

The divinity of Jesus

Despite his presentation of Jesus as a man with very human emotions, Mark is very clear that this is the Son of God. That divinity is revealed most clearly in his battle with the forces of darkness, especially in confrontations with the demonic. It is these demonic powers which are more likely to understand the divine power of Jesus than his immediate followers and who are therefore commanded to be silent. The demons knew who he was (Mark 1:34).

The secrecy theme

All through Mark's Gospel it is clear that Jesus has a clear understanding of where his ministry is leading him. But this knowledge is hidden from the disciples. It is not that Jesus is trying to keep his followers in ignorance but rather that he does not want the forces of darkness to guess at what is to come. The forces of evil are to think that the cross is their victory, unaware that it is actually their greatest undoing.

The abandonment of Jesus

At the moment of death, Jesus is utterly alone. Judas betrays him. Jesus' followers and family have all deserted him. Peter has denied that he even knew him. The symbolic physical darkness echoes the emotional and spiritual abandonment suffered by Jesus. He is mocked by his enemies and apparently deserted even by God. The darkness of the cross is broken only by the moment of death and so the accomplishment of victory. The forces of darkness are given no clue as to the real meaning of the cross until it is too late.

Here Mark faces the essential paradox of the cross. Jesus is fully human but he is also fully divine. A cosmic confrontation with the ultimate powers is being played out in the face of the religious power of the Jewish authorities and the secular power of the occupying force of Rome. There is therefore a power that lies behind both these obvious powers. In other words, the cross is not just an instrument of torture, used by the Jews to rid them of an uncomfortable opponent, or by the Romans to bring a brigand to justice. The real issue lies in the potential of the cross to deal with the cosmic power of evil that lies behind the earthly powers of this world. The resurrection is almost incidental in Mark. It is almost as though the resurrection was an inevitable consequence of the victory over the powers of darkness brought about by the confrontation on the cross rather than an event that sheds light on the cross.

The extent of this confrontation with evil is emphasised by Mark's picture of the darkness that came over the world which is only relieved by the actual death of Jesus (Mark 15:33). At the moment of his death Mark tells us that the curtain of the temple was torn in two from top to bottom. The secret is finally out. The powers of darkness are defeated. The holiness and power of God is released from the temple into the world at the moment of the death of Jesus. While it is certainly true that both Matthew and Luke follow Mark in reporting the darkness that encompassed the earth during the crucifixion and the tearing of the curtain, they are adopting Mark's account, it is not their own original insight.

Matthew – the cross as fulfilment

Matthew's depiction of the cross stands closer to Mark than either of the other two Gospels but even so he offers his own additional perspective. Matthew is known as the Gospel written for the Jews. Such a description is entirely justified in that his community was based in Alexandria where large numbers of Jews lived. We can safely assume that Matthew's church contained far more Jewish converts than Gentile converts as compared with the much more Gentile setting of Mark's audience in Rome.

Jesus as fulfilling Old Testament Scriptures

All the way through the Gospel of Matthew, he makes reference to the fulfilment of Old Testament Scriptures in the birth, life and death of Jesus. Sometimes Matthew is content to follow Mark's account, which had already begun to echo Old Testament references. For example, the division of Jesus' clothes by throwing lots, which fulfils Psalm 22:18, is found in Mark. On other occasions Matthew includes material not found in Mark which clearly reflects Old Testament passages, without actually drawing attention to the fact that this was a direct fulfilment of Scripture, for example, the presence of the two thieves which connects the death of Jesus with Isaiah 53:12. In other passages, Matthew makes the direct point that a particular event occurred specifically in order that Scripture might be fulfilled, for example, the payment by Judas of thirty pieces of silver. Matthew tells us that this was to fulfil the words of Jeremiah (Matthew 27:9).

Jesus as the king who ushers in the kingdom

For Matthew, Jesus is the long-promised king. He emphasises the royal genealogy of Jesus in the birth narratives. The wise men come to look for the king of the Jews. Even at his birth, Herod sees a potential rival in the baby Jesus. In the trial before Pilate, Jesus accepts the same title, king of the Jews. The ascription as king is placed on the cross itself. But what kind of king is this? The title fixed to his cross was intended as an insult. Matthew uses the insult to draw attention to the true nature of his kingship. Following the resurrection, Jesus makes the claim that now all power in heaven and on earth has been given to him. This was no ordinary king and no ordinary kingdom. The cross is the means by which the king is enthroned and the kingdom can be announced and established.

Jesus as the founder of the Church

In keeping with his Jewish audience, Matthew emphasises two other aspects of the ministry of Jesus. He was above all a teacher, the one who gave the sermon on the mount, a new set of commandments from another mountain which fulfilled and explained all that Moses had previously brought to Israel. This new teaching was not designed to set aside the law but to fulfil the law. Matthew seems to be particularly harsh with the scribes and Pharisees, not because of their devotion to the law but more because of the way in which they had undermined its good purpose. By over-emphasising the law as a legal code they had missed the true spirit and intent which underlay it. The teaching of Jesus therefore properly explains the law rather than simply ends it.

Matthew makes the connection between Jesus the teacher of the law and the establishment of the new Israel, the Church. Alone among the Gospel writers, Matthew speaks of the Church, its foundation and its importance. The cross marks the boundary point at which the new Israel finally comes into being. Following the crucifixion and the resurrection, the Church has both a mandate to preach and baptise but also to make disciples, that is, to live as the new Israel. For Matthew therefore, the cross fulfils the Old Testament hopes of Israel and marks the coming of the kingdom. That kingdom is intimately connected with the community of the new Israel – the Church. The cross therefore founds the Church to such an extent that the Church could be called the community of the cross, the suffering servant founds the suffering community.

Luke – the cross as reconciliation

As with Matthew, Luke begins with the material that he takes from Mark's Gospel but his perspective on the cross offers an important additional insight. For Luke, the theme of the love of God is an extraordinarily powerful element in his Gospel account. That theme is worked out in a number of ways.

The sick are healed

Clearly Luke the physician has an interest in the healing work of Jesus. As many commentators have noted, Luke gives particular mention to such healing accounts. But Luke is not just acting out of medical curiosity. He sees the healing of the sick as evidence of the compassion of Jesus and so of the love of God.

The lost are special

For Luke, those who stand outside the kingdom of God, the lost, are of particular interest. For example, in Luke 15, the whole chapter is taken up with three parables, each of which is dedicated to an exploration of the importance of finding the lost and the joy in heaven which comes when that which is lost is found. The evident joy of the heavenly father, the willingness (as in the case of the prodigal son) of the father to even endure disgrace as he looks anxiously for the restoration of his son, are indications of the vastness of the love of God.

Forgiveness is offered

The offer of forgiveness and so the reality of reconciliation with God particularly interests Luke. He alone of all the evangelists, tells the story of the prodigal son with its emphasis on forgiveness and of costly, unconditional reconciliation. To the alert eye, that same story is also a metaphor for the death and resurrection of Jesus. The younger son, having realised his desperate state says, 'I will arise and go to my father.' His father replies to the disapproving older son by saying, 'For this son of mine was dead and is alive again.' The linking of a theme of forgiveness with that of death and resurrection is further emphasised in Luke's own passion narrative. In Luke's account Jesus offers words of forgiveness from the cross. The cross is an enactment of forgiving love. The dying Jesus on the cross offers the certainty of reconciliation with God to the thief beside him – 'today you will be with me in paradise'. The love of God is presented by Luke as amazingly inclusive. The cross has a universal significance for all peoples. The marginalised are particularly included. Women, the poor, sinners of all descriptions are the special recipients of the attention of Jesus. For Luke, the cosmic dimensions of the cross emphasised by Mark are brought to bear on the very human condition of individuals in need of healing, forgiveness and so reconciliation. Repentance is the proper response of individuals who hear the message. There is no need to wait hopefully for an ultimate judgement on the last day. The standing of individuals before God can be viewed hopefully in the light of the compassion of God for the lost. Repentance is certainly required of the individual but it is not the repentance that flows from despair at wrongdoing so much as a joyful revelation of the astonishing love of God.

Mark presents the centurion at the cross as declaring, 'Surely this man is the Son of God?' The response of awe at the sight of cosmic events unfolding becomes for Luke a response to the possibility of being made right with God. Luke's centurion says, 'Surely this was a righteous man?' As Smail suggests:

If 'righteous' in this context has its full biblical meaning, denoting not just personal innocence but the ability to make things right, then the Lukan centurion has more evident grounds for his verdict than the Markan counterpart, because in the Gospel according to Luke that is exactly what Jesus is doing from the cross.[2]

For Luke, the cross represents the continued and necessary activity of the ministry of Jesus, not a moment of crisis as in Mark, or the decisive point at which the new Israel comes into being as in Matthew.

John – the triumph of the cross

John's Gospel presents Jesus from the very beginning of his ministry as the lamb of God. John the Baptist announces Jesus as 'the lamb of God'. The designation of Jesus as a lamb carries with it a deep significance that resonates from the whole history of the people of Israel. The dispute between Cain and Abel centred on the desire of God to be worshipped by the sacrifice of a lamb. Abraham was prevented by God from sacrificing his only son and instead a sheep was offered in his place. By contrast, Jesus as the paschal lamb, God's only Son, was not spared from death on the cross. The blood of a lamb was used to protect the people of God at the time of the original Passover at the time of Moses. To call Jesus the lamb of God was to call into play the religious imagination of the people of Israel and to declare something of the meaning of his ministry.

The victory of the cross

With this Old Testament background in mind, the cross for John was the triumphant completion of the ministry of

Jesus. The darkness of the synoptic Gospels is absent in John. The cry 'It is finished' is less a cry of loneliness than a cry of achievement. The task has been accomplished. The potential tragedy of the cross becomes a source of wonder and anticipation. Jesus may seem to be a helpless victim but from the perspective of John he is actually in control of the situation, not being condemned to death by a judicial process so much as judging the world from the cross. His death on a cross, or lifting up, is a means of drawing all men to himself (John 12: 31–33).

The redeeming power of the cross

The judgement that flows from the cross is not concerned with condemnation so much as with redemption. The cross contains within it the power to put right all of the wrongs of the world, to allow a new beginning in which relationship with God and so relationships between human beings can be recast. John does not spell out in detail how this is to happen but rather places the events of the cross in the context of a cosmic and universal drama. For John, the last supper is a foretaste of the heavenly banquet and the cross a means of taking the very human interactions of the Passover meal and infusing them with real meaning. The bread and wine of the final meal with his disciples become now the body and blood of Jesus. Without the cross the elements of the last supper are entirely without power. With the cross these simple elements become a genuine means of communion with God, a Eucharist which connects Calvary with the last things.

The gift of the Spirit

Unlike the synoptic Gospels, John makes a strong connection between the actual events of the passion with the
giving of the Spirit. Whereas in the Luke/Acts account,
the Spirit is sent after the ascension of Jesus, John suggests
that the Spirit was breathed on the disciples during the
intimate moments during Jesus' self-revelation to them
following the resurrection. He makes a further connection
between the actual death of Jesus on the cross and the
giving of the Spirit. In finally giving up his spirit on the
cross he allows the Holy Spirit of God to come and fill the
tiny community still gathered around the foot of the cross.
As Smail suggests, 'From the cross he gave the disciple
company the Spirit who makes all things new, the Spirit
that is symbolised as always in this Gospel by the water
that pours from his side with the blood of his self-giving
when his body is pierced by the soldier's spear.'[3]

So for John, the cross has both universal and cosmic
significance; but his picture is not so much that of a battle
with the forces of darkness as a unifying of this world with
the next. The triumph of the cross is not so much the cry
of victory as the celebration of healing. All are being
restored to their proper place as a consequence of the
cross. A new community of love is being founded. Gentle,
forbearing, forgiveness is to be the quality of that which
has been placed by the Spirit in the emerging company of
disciples. The feeding of sheep (in the sense of the com-
mandment given to Peter), will be as important as the
declaration of the need to repent. The cross therefore
heals and restores all it touches.

A ransom for many

It should be clear as we review the four pictures presented by Mark, Matthew, Luke and John, that these are not four different views of the cross, still less are they four conflicting views. The shades of emphasis merely add to a core understanding that the cross was somehow vital for the cosmos, for humanity, and for individuals. Such is its importance that the mission and message of the Church flow from a conscious awareness of the centrality of the cross. For all of the Gospel writers, the cross did something, it accomplished something, it has changed all things to such an extent that it came to be seen as an essential part of the purpose for Christ's coming. It might be too blunt to say that he was born only in order that he may die, but still the truth is not far from such a crude formulation.

Most scholars agree that Mark's report of the words of Jesus prior to the triumphal entry represent a very early understanding of the significance of the death of Jesus. 'For even the Son of Man did not come to be served, but to serve, and to give his life as a ransom for many' (Mark 10:45). The idea of Jesus dying in the place of others, or in this case for many, was a new idea for the Jewish community. Certainly there was an idea that suffering could have a purpose in expiating sins. Suffering therefore could be creative and freeing, especially if that suffering was for God. There was also the idea that animal sacrifice could be made in order to deal with wrongdoing or sin. Even more, the Old Testament contained the notion that the Son of Man would be pre-ordained to die.

However, there is no explicit Jewish tradition that the death of the Son of Man would be directed particularly towards the wiping out of sin, of expiatory death, of being a ransom for others. This specifically Christian declaration of the significance of the death of Jesus could have emerged either in the teaching of Jesus to the early community or in their own reflection in the power of the Spirit on the death of Jesus.[4] However it arose, whether by a creative interaction between the older Jewish traditions that they had inherited or by the direct post-resurrection teaching of the risen Lord, it is this single contention that forms the basis for the Christian message. The cross is not a tragedy but a crucial part of God's purpose for his Son and for his world.

But the common conviction of all the Gospel writers that the death of Christ was for many, indeed for all, is declared not explained. However, St Paul, in his various epistles does attempt a more detailed explanation of that central reality and it is to his understanding of the cross that we must now turn.

Questions

1. Why do you think each Gospel writer gives so much space to their various accounts of the passion story?
2. In what way do you think that the cross has defeated the powers of darkness?
3. Does the cross act as a judgement on the people of Israel and does it give Israel's life added meaning?
4. Does the cross end the ministry of Jesus or extend it and how would you illustrate your answer?
5. In what ways can the cross act as an event with the power to heal communities and individuals?

Notes

1. William Barclay, *The Daily Study Bible, Gospel of*

Matthew, Volume I, St Andrew's Press, Glasgow, 1960, p.xviii.
2. Tom Smail, p.25.
3. *Ibid.*, p.26.
4. Pannenberg extensively discusses this issue in *Jesus, God and Man*, p.248.

3

The Cross and the Mission of Paul

The cross of Jesus cries out for an explanation and St Paul was the very first Christian thinker to give what we might call a doctrinal account of why Jesus died. This chapter outlines why Paul undertook such a task, the audience he was addressing, and the concerns he had. It also gives the main contours of his answer to the question.

The Cross and the Mission of Paul

When television sets were significantly less available than they are today, viewing was something of a community experience. I can remember watching a slightly fuzzy black-and-white screen in the home of my best friend. As a ten year old, the programmes with the greatest fascination were those with the highest body count – usually westerns. We all know that real death is nothing like the events of the small screen or the silver screen. In film fantasy the deaths of the bad guys are occasions for cheers and the death of heroes moments of melancholic pride. On film it is easy to die for a cause. Today, even the cinema acknowledges that in real life death can be tragic, painful, pointless, messy and frightening.

The death of Jesus on a cross cried out for an explanation. He was not a hero in the sense that he was dying for an ideological end. Curiously it was just such a man, Jesus Barabbas – a freedom fighter, who was freed instead of Jesus the son of Joseph. What then did his death mean? The Gospels all present the fact of Jesus' death and declare its meaning in terms of a ransom, a death for all of us. Such an explanation is cast entirely in the context of the history of the people of Israel. It becomes meaningful against the background of such a shared understanding. Those who were familiar with the history of Israel, the tradition of temple sacrifice, of expiation for sins, could more easily appreciate the significance of the death of Jesus as the ultimate paschal lamb.

To a greater or lesser extent, the four Gospel writers reflected a tradition that was in touch with the culture of the synagogue. The earliest converts and missionaries had all been Jews and many of the earliest Gentile converts were from that circle of the 'god-fearers' who were well acquainted with Jewish custom and tradition. The story of Jesus was faithfully recounted by the four Gospel writers who were trying hard to reflect an earlier oral tradition that had developed in a Jewish milieu. The story the evangelists portrayed was not systematically explained even if the way they told the story suggests to us their own understanding of the story.

Paul the missionary

The apostle Paul was also in touch with that same early tradition. Despite the attempts of some writers to suggest that somehow Paul was a later interloper, misunderstanding and somehow changing the gospel message, we need to constantly remember that Paul was converted in the very first few years of the Christian community. He was himself a Jew, some of his relatives had been believers before him (Romans 16) and although it is merely speculation, they may even have known Jesus during his earthly ministry. At the very least we can be sure that Paul knew many if not all of the first apostles and was well acquainted with James the brother of Jesus. Paul was well taught by those who certainly did understand the message of the early Church and, given his own theological training as a Pharisee, he was well equipped to perceive the significance of the message in a Jewish context. But Paul was a missionary whose vocation meant that he had to offer an explanation for the death of Jesus in terms that could transcend the purely cultural and religious context of the Jewish people.

The radical nature of his enterprise began with his immersion in the creative atmosphere of the Church in Antioch. As far as we can tell Antioch was the most Gentile of all the churches in the very early apostolic period. The conversion of so many Gentiles seems to have been rather unexpected and it soon became evident that a number of new unconsidered problems emerged for the early Church. These were sufficiently thorny that the leaders in Antioch realised that the debate needed to involve the whole Church and so the symbolic centre of the Christian community, the Church in Jerusalem, was consulted.

Given the high quality of the leadership in Antioch, it does not take much imagination to see that the reason for taking the debate to Jerusalem was not because the Church in Antioch lacked theological and pastoral resources. They were certainly able to offer a creative solution to the dilemma they faced. It was precisely because they were good theologians that they had seen what was at stake. This was not what it appeared to be on the surface, namely a difficult pastoral issue – do Gentiles need to be circumcised? The underlying issue inevitably asked questions about the very nature of the gospel message itself.

From the perspective of the missionary task, the question was the tender and provocative matter as to whether

Gentiles needed to be Jews first in order to be Christians. To those of us standing two millennia away from the solution, the answer seems obvious. But to a community which was predominantly Jewish in membership and entirely Jewish in terms of its religious heritage and self-understanding, the answer was not at all so obvious. Why should these Gentiles not become Jews in ritual terms in order to enjoy the benefits of the new Israel? Surely, if there was to be no immersion in all that it meant to be Jewish, the full significance of being part of the Messianic community – a Christian – would be watered down and eventually lost. This was not a straightforward matter at all.

The heart of the gospel

Why then did the Jewish Church in Jerusalem even con-template taking the momentous decision that they did in suggesting that Gentiles might enjoy all the benefits of the new covenant without embracing the commitments of the old covenant? We can speculate that this was solely and entirely the guidance of the Holy Spirit. We might wonder if there was the very human consideration that the Church in Antioch was seen as a minor aberration which would soon disappear in the context of the expectation of the imminent return of the Lord.

But from Paul's perspective the issue was absolutely clear. If it was necessary for someone to become a Jew first in order to become a Christian then the death of Christ on the cross was of no value. In short, Christ had died in vain. This then was more than just a missionary problem to do with the cultural clothing of the gospel. It was not about externals but about the nature of the gospel itself. Paul saw that if one could not be saved except by undergoing what he later called 'the mutilation of the flesh' (circumcision) then inevitably it was the act of becoming a Jew that played a significant part in one's salvation. For Paul it was the death of Christ on a cross, and that alone, which could bring salvation. All other religious initiation and ritual had to be subjected to the judgement and power of the cross. It was not possible for the message of the cross to be made a mere addendum to the process of becoming a Jew.

This was the issue that lay at the centre of Paul's message to the Galatians. Paul had some very hard words for the good folks in the Galatian Church. He accused those who had been circumcised as 'falling away from grace'. He goes even further and says that if they allow themselves to be circumcised, 'Christ will be of no value to you at all.' The critic of Paul might object that this seems rather harsh. Why not let them indulge in some additional ritual if they feel it to be helpful? After all, some like to fast, in other ages some Christians have undergone a variety of physical hardships in order to help their spiritual discipline. Isn't this just such an issue? Why is Paul making such hard work of a relatively small point? Why not live and let live? Is this simply a matter of competition for disciples? Is Paul worried about losing position and support in the Church?

Not at all; Paul has grasped something of tremendous importance. It is not the act of circumcision that matters here. As Paul points out neither circumcision nor un-circumcision has any intrinsic value of its own. It is the significance which is being invested in circumcision that concerns Paul. The Galatians are looking at circumcision in terms of its contribution to their salvation. The 'Judai-sers' have convinced them that to place their faith in Christ's death on a cross is not enough. They will not receive salvation without circumcision. Paul rightly sees that this is not just an additional and unnecessary burden but it immediately takes such believers to a place where they have to obey every law, not just the law of circumcision. He rightly asks, why then has Christ died?

This thunderbolt of a theological revolution came first as a consequence of reflection in the face of missionary praxis. In short, a practical problem forced Paul to consider the heart of his message. It is interesting that nowhere does Paul offer a pragmatic solution to the problem of the Gentiles. He might for example have argued that baptism stood for circumcision and therefore by baptism one became a Jew and hence a Christian. He saw that to offer a purely pragmatic compromise failed to take account of the nature of the Christian message. From hereon, the message of Paul was centred entirely on the Christ as the crucified God. Once Paul had seen that the cross and the crucified Christ could not be separated in terms of the message of the gospel it also became clear that all other doctrines needed to be understood in the light of this core reality. It is not possible for us to consider the full extent of Paul's thought but a few areas will illustrate the extent to which his thinking about the cross dominated all else.

The nature of God

For Paul, the cross offers a profound insight into the nature of God. It is not just that he sees God as the one who has taken an initiative in the affairs of men by sending Jesus, nor even that the sacrifice of his only Son demonstrates the extent of his love. The message of the cross goes deeper still. In using the cross as a means of bringing reconciliation, God necessarily rejects any other means of salvation. In particular, he deliberately, knowingly, lays aside his power and opts for weakness.

The cross therefore is not a defeat which demonstrates God's lack of power or inability to obtain his own way in the face of the powers of this world. Instead the cross is a victory which shows that the power of God lies in his astonishing willingness to lay aside all power of coercion. God seeks to bring humanity into relationship with himself by the simple power of sacrificial love. This is the power of a relationship which is even willing to experience disgrace in order to draw men and women into a new community of love.

As a result of the cross, men and women are called into the way of the cross. Just as Jesus has laid aside his majesty and power, so Christians are called to exercise their own power in weakness. It is not difficult to see how this message had a revolutionary application in the highly stratified context of Roman society. For the many powerless in society, Paul's message of the cross presented a picture of their important participation in a new society. Indeed one of the striking images of the early Church is precisely the extent to which social barriers were transcended. Such an outcome is all the more remarkable when one remembers that in Roman society, each social group often had its own distinct cult.

The appeal to weakness is one which Paul sets out in his own ministry. It is because of the way of the cross that Paul is not willing to use intrigue, coercion or indeed any underhanded means in order to obtain his own way. Paul offers his own weakness in adversity as an illustration of the power of the gospel. The apparent foolishness of the cross is contrasted with the wisdom of this world which prefers to use power manipulatively to obtain its own way. The powers of this world are defeated by a God who refuses to use power in the way that they understand it. Thus the moment of God's greatest defeat actually represents an ultimate victory for the new way of love.

The plan of salvation

From this perspective of God's laying down of power, Paul is able to reinterpret the whole history of Israel in terms of the plan of salvation that God has in mind for the world. The immediate context for Paul's re-evaluation of the significance of the history of Israel lay in the competing ideologies of first-century Palestine. The ruling class represented by the chief priests saw the survival of the temple worship as the most important matter. For them, the history of Israel could only be understood in terms of what took place in the ritual of the temple. God was present in the temple and for them the history of Israel could only be understood in terms of the survival of the temple.

By contrast, the Pharisees saw the proper application of the law as the legitimate inheritance of the Old Testament message. For this group, God's law was his gift to the world and the preservation of the law and its contemporary application was the essential task. The radicals, represented by the zealots, believed that the lesson of the Old Testament could best be understood in terms of military victory and by this means, the establishment of a territorial integrity – the promised land. Even a scant survey of Old Testament Scriptures allows one to see how each of these groups could draw such diverse lessons from the same essential document.

But Paul suggests that all three groups have misunderstood the Old Testament. For him, the real lesson lies in the recurrent message that it is faith in God that marks out the authentic people of God. His case centres on the faith of

Abraham. Paul rightly points out that it was a combination of faith and obedience that caused God to be pleased with Abraham, not an observance of a law given to Moses or a land given at the time of Aaron or a temple at the time of Solomon. The true sons and daughters of Abraham are not the circumcised but those who have faith.

Why is faith so important? Paul's answer is that faith in the Old Testament points always towards the cross. In this sense the gospel is already present in the faith of Abraham. Faith inevitably involves the laying down of personal power in favour of a reliance on the very different power of God. For Paul, God always acts differently than human beings. The cross demonstrates this essential reality.

The law

Once Paul had asserted the primary place of faith in the plan of God he necessarily had to deal with the purpose of the law of God. He was not willing to say that the law was a kind of aberration, either a mistaken action of God or a misunderstanding on the part of Moses. The law had a clear purpose which could only now be properly understood in the light of the cross. Clearly, this was a sensitive subject, not just because of the Judaisers who wanted to uphold the place of the law in the newly emerging Christian communities but also because many Jewish Christians were understandably reluctant to abandon their observance of the law. The problem is clearly illustrated by the difficulty that Peter had when commanded in a dream to kill and eat that which he considered to be ritually impure.

The law was not bad but its purpose needed to be rethought. Paul argued that the purpose of the law was not to bring men and women into a right relationship with

God but rather to demonstrate the reality of sin and so point out the gulf between humanity and God. In other words, the law was an aid to conscience, a means of perceiving the holiness of God. The law clearly indicated the problem for which the cross was the proper and only solution. The law therefore was good but it could never act as the basis for a new community, the life of the new people of God. Only the cross could do that.

Baptism and Lord's Supper

The cross not only allowed a re-evaluation of all the rituals of the past (the law), it also offered a means of understanding the new rituals of the Christian Church. Therefore baptism needed to be understood as a representation of the uniting of believers with Christ. The waters of baptism represented the death of Christ. Coming out of the water represented the resurrection of Christ. For Paul, this was crucial in order to prevent Christian baptism becoming only a new ritual cleansing. If salvation was brought about simply by the act of being baptised then the sacrament of baptism was in danger of replacing the work of the cross rather than incorporating Christ's action on the cross in the life of the believer. In the same way, the Lord's supper represented for Christians the death of Christ on the cross. The bread represented the body of Christ on the cross. The cup represented the cup of suffering. The wine stood for the blood of Christ. In this way, participation in the Eucharist did not in itself bring salvation, rather it connected believers with the act of salvation brought about by the cross itself.

The mystery of the cross

In making the cross so completely central to his message, it is important to emphasise that Paul was not creating a new message, different in some important respects to the message that was already being proclaimed by the whole Christian community. Rather, Paul was attempting to clearly explain the meaning of the narrative already in circulation. Not only did he attempt to remain completely true to that existing narrative, he also used images which were already in the vocabulary and imagination of the Christian community. However, we see in Paul's writings a fuller account of these images.

It is certainly true that his use of these existing images was creative. Why did he feel it necessary to explain the meaning of these terms to his audiences? In very simple terms, it is clear that he could see that the cross represented a profound mystery. By mystery I do not mean something that is unintelligible or even worse something that makes no sense. Mystery used in this sense means something that can never be fully comprehended but which can be apprehended. The common way to apprehend any mystery is to approach it by using a number of examples or metaphors. In other words it is possible to say that this mystery is like something else that we can know.

In seeking to explain the mystery of the cross to cultures beyond that of Jewish people, Paul took four key concepts and attempted to relate them to ideas that were commonplace in everyday life. The underlying theme in all of these images is that of substitution. In other words, viewed from a number of perspectives Christ died in our place, or on our behalf.

Propitiation

This language is taken from the world of religion, but it is not just the Christian faith that has a concept of propitiation. It was certainly a common idea in Judaism and indeed in many of the religious cults that were widespread in the Roman Empire. The key notion is that a sacrifice is made in order to turn away the proper anger of God, in very simple terms to placate God or the gods. This can be a very crude idea which might seem almost barbaric to many. Certainly the idea that the gods or spirits of a place could be satisfied by a simple offering, either of food or possessions or an animal or even a person, has been a commonplace notion in the animistic religions that Christianity has often replaced. Is this then an appropriate way to understand the death of Jesus?

The Christian application of this idea does not depend on the thought that God is specifically angry because of a particular sin and therefore needs to be placated from time to time. Rather, the idea begins with the awareness that God is angry because of the total impact that the sin of humanity has on his world. Sin or injustice is always felt most acutely by the helpless – the poor, the weak and the defenceless. This is why the Old Testament speaks out so clearly against those who practise injustice of any kind.

Paul's case is that a just God could no longer stand by and see evil perpetrated on a humanity he loves. God's nature is to be both just and loving and these two parts of his nature are brought together in the cross. The reality of evil in the world is directly confronted by Christ's death on the cross. God's anger over wrongdoing is satisfied because a proper propitiation is made for the evil which has been done. This is not just a case of an angry God seeking someone, anyone, on whom to visit his wrath. The one on the cross is himself God. In seeking redress for the wrongs of humanity, God takes the punishment upon himself.

Redemption

The idea of Jesus as a redeemer of humanity is related to the phrase used by Mark – Jesus died as a ransom for many. Ransom and redemption are terms taken originally from the marketplace. Both words convey a sense that a given commodity has a specific value which can be exchanged, often in a bartering situation, for another commodity or set of goods which are believed by both parties to have an equal value.

At a very basic level the notion of ransom is commonly used to describe the taking of human hostages. In such a situation a particular person's life is given a value and they are held to ransom for the required payment. This is certainly an ancient tradition but one which still operates in many parts of our contemporary world. As we are all aware, there is no single price for every human being. The crude marketplace which deals in human lives recognises that the price an individual is marked by is a combination of the willingness of others to save the person's life and the actual ability to pay.

In the thinking of the Christian community all human flesh was held captive by the impact of evil. In popular imagery humankind was held captive by the devil and as such was powerless to have a proper and free relationship with God. Paul suggests that the life of Jesus represented a value or price which was so great that it was a sufficient price to allow the whole of humanity to be freed from the captivity of sin, evil and death. The risen Jesus is therefore both Lord and God. In particular he is Lord of the Church and has bought with his own blood the freedom of all those who seek to live under his Lordship in the community of the Church. We are redeemed by the blood of the lamb.

Justification

The term justification came originally from the world of the law. It was a legal term which meant that someone who had been justified was innocent in the eyes of the law. Their position had been justified or vindicated and so there was no further case to argue. They could go free and no penalty could be applied to them. We know from the New Testament that Paul was well acquainted with both Jewish and Roman law. Arguably this is the image that most appeals to Paul as an explanation of the cross.

For Paul, the cross demonstrates the astonishing grace of God. By taking the punishment that was due to be ours, Jesus answers the case against us, on our behalf. We are now therefore legally free, the law (in this case the law of God) cannot condemn us any more. We are justified entirely by our faith in God, not by any action of our own. Christ's death on the cross accomplishes this work of justification. In this sense we are justified by the blood of Jesus.

Reconciliation

The idea of reconciliation comes more generally from the world of human, social relationships. This is entirely appropriate in that Paul's notion of the reconciliation brought about by the cross is not just a matter of being reconciled to God, important though that may be. Paul's point is that our individual reconciliation with God opens up the door to a wider social reconciliation. The cross acts as a way of healing.

This is the purpose of the atonement, to be at one with God, to have made peace with him and so to be at peace with the whole of creation. Access to God opens up the way for peace to extend to the whole of society. Thus the cross of Christ allows social divisions to be overcome. There is now no longer a division between Jew, Greek and barbarian, nor between men and women, rich and poor, weak and strong. All are made one because of the reconciling power of the cross.

The motif of reconciliation is used by Paul to emphasise that we are not merely beneficiaries of the cross but we are also called to be ambassadors of the cross. Christians are to demonstrate the power of the cross in the new communities of the cross that are being established across the world, but also to declare the good news of the cross to any who might listen. It is entirely appropriate that having been forced by his mission to consider the significance of the cross, Paul's explanation of the meaning of the cross always led him back to the mission itself. That same challenge faces the contemporary Christian community. We are constantly called to think afresh about the meaning of the cross so that the mission of reconciliation can properly go forward. The images used by Paul may not all be helpful for our contemporary situation. What matters, however, is not the images themselves so much as the underlying reality that they seek to communicate.

Having seen how Paul sought to interpret the story of the cross to his audience we need now to turn to the underlying concepts that the cross seeks to demonstrate. Once we can be clear about the ideas contained in the notion of atonement we can attempt to think through how we might communicate to our contemporary audience.

Questions

1. Why did Paul insist that the message of the cross was of more importance than any other aspect of Christian belief and practise?
2. Does the cross reveal God's lack of power in dealing with evil and its effects? In short, did the cross in fact represent the failure of the mission of Jesus?
3. Why is faith more important to Paul than any other factor?
4. Is God ever angry and if so how might we describe that anger?
5. What images from ordinary life might we use to convey the meaning of the cross today?

4

A Sacrificial Death

This chapter explores the meaning of sacrifice and specifically its relationship with the core meanings that we give to life. In this context we begin to explore the nature of evil and the notion of sin. What do these concepts mean and how does the cross address them?

A Sacrificial Death

Crisis, danger and adversity seem to produce unlikely heroes of many kinds. The common testimony of many of those we recognise as acting heroically tells us that they did what came naturally. They did not think they were doing anything unusual at the time. Despite an obvious risk to their own lives, they acted to save the lives of others as a spontaneous response. The element of personal danger causes us to respond to their heroism with bravery awards of one kind or another. We are grateful for their unselfish acts.

Often, these spontaneous acts of courage take place when the lives of comrades, friends, family members or loved ones are at risk. Just occasionally there are astonishing acts of sacrifice which go beyond these natural boundaries. Two such stories emanate from the horrors of the Second World War.

Mother Maria was a Russian nun, a mother superior in charge of a convent, when the Second World War broke out. Knowing of the plight of Jewish people she gave instructions for the convent to be used as a hiding place for Jewish

71

fugitives. Eventually, the inevitable discovery of her activity took place and she, together with the other nuns, was taken to a concentration camp. Mother Maria was sent to the camp at Ravensbrook. Near the conclusion of the war, the mass killings of the Jewish prisoners began. On one occasion, Mother Maria noticed a young Jewish woman, weeping hysterically with fear and anguish. Seeing her distress, Mother Maria quietly offered to take her place in the line and die instead of her. It was Good Friday 1945.[1]

The concentration camp at Auschwitz witnessed a very similar sacrificial act much earlier in the same conflict. In July 1941 a number of prisoners escaped and to discourage other such attempts it was announced that ten prisoners, chosen at random, were to die. The ten were to be placed in a starvation chamber and forced to die an agonisingly slow death. The ten were chosen and one man was overcome with grief. He shouted for mercy. He was young and had a young family that he desperately wished to see again. A Roman Catholic priest, Maximilian Kolbe offered to die in his place. Exactly fifty years later, the death of Maximilian Kolbe was marked by the Pope at a ceremony in the Vatican Square. Among the crowd of 150,000 stood the man he replaced, Francis Gajowniczek. Standing beside Francis was his wife, his children and his many grandchildren. Pope John Paul II made the clear connection between the sacrificial action of Maximilian and the death of Jesus on the cross.[2]

Nearly every story of selfless sacrifice produces a mixture of emotions in most of us. Admiration and astonishment combine with the inevitable silent question as to whether we would act in the same way in similar circumstances. We probably feel that we would not do so, which is precisely why such events are seen as newsworthy, remarkable and heroic. Yet, even though we might feel unsure of our own actions in such situations, we can understand and recognise what is taking place. Generosity of this kind is not a mystery even if it is unusual.

The death of Jesus contains many of the ingredients of these stories of self-sacrifice. He was betrayed and yet did not defend himself. His death was that of an innocent in the face of evil. Even in the agonies of death his words were those of forgiveness and not condemnation, of love and compassion, not hatred and revenge. This was certainly the death of a hero. But who or what was he dying for? The Gospels are clear that he was dying for many. Paul asserts that Jesus died for all humanity and not just those of his own generation but for those living in all times. How can the death of one man carry such a weight?

One response that comes to us from the Scriptures and from Christian tradition is to answer that the death of Jesus represents a particular kind of sacrificial death. Just what kind of sacrifice needs some exploration and such a trail properly begins with a consideration of the core meaning of sacrifice.

The response of the heart

In thinking about the origins of sacrificial practice we are inevitably led to ask some fundamental questions about the meaning of our existence. Modern science has asked the 'how' questions surrounding human and material origins. Fascinating as these answers might be, reaching as they do to the first few seconds following the 'big bang', they do not address any of the existential 'why' questions that flow from our simply being here. Radical secularists such as Richard Dawkins usually respond that the 'why' questions simply do not matter and therefore should not be asked. That kind of blanket blindness, the refusal to even allow the question to be asked, has never been able to extinguish such natural interest in the majority of humankind.

We can quickly detect at least three basic responses to our existence, all of which can be said to have a religious quality to them. The first is that of wonder. There is a certain quality of childlikeness or innocence that is intrinsically part of such a feeling. Adults are only too aware that the pressures of earning a living, of fractured relationships, of unrealised dreams and of painful personal experiences, act to obscure the sense of wonder in relation to the world in which we live. Yet despite these pressures, there are moments in which that basic sense of wonder returns to remind us of another world, one which we seek to find.

For many, such moments are associated with the natural world – the reminder of beauty. But what matters is not the experience of beauty itself. The same experience can also come from the ecstatic moment in the encounter with music and the arts more widely. The natural world or the arts act as icons to point us past the immediate to the world of wonder beyond. We become aware that we are not just observers living in a semi-detached relationship to our world. It is not just that we are alive and so able to observe, we are also vital partakers in a living universe. To engage in wonder is to wish to recognise that which is greater than us with some kind of sacrificial act.

The sense of wonder is closely related to the second basic response, that of gratitude. Some years ago, I climbed a mountain in the Isle of Arran, just off the west coast of Scotland. Unusually for Scotland it was a hot summer's day and the heather was in full bloom. Even at a good altitude, the insects were active and the climb was sticky and slow. The summit brought an astonishing reward, a view of the surrounding landscape but more particularly the sea as I had never seen it before in that part of the world. The ocean was a deep blue with the currents clearly marked as lighter trails, weaving a clear but complex pattern. This was a moment of awe and joy, of sheer uninhibited pleasure at the privilege of witnessing such a scene.

The downward journey was further rewarded by a plunge into a deep pool of cooling, sparkling mountain water. This was an experience of knowing that I was not just living in this world, I was a grateful partaker of its gifts. The sense of gratitude, the feeling that life is a gift from a higher power forms part of that ancient response of wonder that sees a sacrificial offering as a very basic desire to engage in a natural act of thanksgiving. We live and we are glad that we do.

A third response relates to a deep awareness that although life contains the potential for awe and that we can be glad to live in this world, life is also precarious. The daily awareness of living close to extinction was clearly greater for those ancient agricultural communities responsible for producing their own food or for hunter-gatherer societies always dependent on finding food. Vulnerability to the forces of nature beyond the control of any human community induced a deep appreciation of the importance of fertility and the blessing of a bountiful harvest. The culmination of a successful hunt produced the same kind of feelings. The consequences of failure could be literally terminal.

The sense of an immediate dependence on the earth and its fruits has been replaced by a more general consciousness of the precarious nature of life. At a personal level, those we know die. For parents, the illness of a child immediately emphasises the limits of human ingenuity

and the frailty of life. In a more general sense we are aware
that the twentieth century has witnessed the introductions
of hazards previously unknown.

For the first time in human history we are able to
destroy all of life in an increasingly bewildering range of
approaches. Germ warfare can be added to nuclear warfare as an effective means of ending the life of whole
communities. Added to the spectre of new diseases has
come the danger of ecological damage to planet earth
together with the unforeseeable outcomes of genetically
manipulated food and species. These recent developments
mean that we cannot feel too certain about the future
prospects for humanity.

A sense that life is tenuous can produce a wide range of
responses. One of those responses could be described as
the need to offer a sacrificial offering to guard against the
vicissitudes of life. At the most basic level, many acts of
superstition are unconscious acts of safeguarding oneself
against unforeseen and undesirable consequences. Religious acts of sacrificial offering, especially the offering of
the first fruits, basic in many primal religions, represents a
more conscious response to the same existential concern.

The response of religion

We can see from a brief examination of our human response
to the world in which we live that there is an easy and
natural connection between that response and the desire
to make a sacrificial act, whether formal or informal. But
such natural desires do not exhaust the meaning and significance of the place of sacrifice in most religions. We need
also to understand three deeper elements contained within
the concept and practice of sacrifice.

A celebration of life itself

The feeling of gratitude and wonder at the gift of life is clearly important as a starting point, but the celebration of life drives deeper than such feelings. An awareness of the complexity of life and its intimate relationship with the universe suggests that life and death are not simply two polar opposites. Rather there is a relationship between these two elements. In the natural world, life can be renewed through death. Sacrifice is therefore partly an attempt to ensure that the cycle of renewal continues.

The religious significance of the action is seen in the specific linkage between the continued bringing of life from death with the divine origin of life itself. Sacrifice seeks to infuse our ordinary mortal life with the ongoing life of the divine. The sacrifice of a gift seeks to declare that what really matters is the divine spark in all things. The mortal gift is offered to the immortal in recognition of the proper order of reality so bringing a constant realignment of the mortal with the more important immortal.

A connection or fellowship with the author of life

The deeper motivation for this realignment was to unite the giver and receiver in a profound and fundamental fellowship. In the context of the people of Israel, sacrifice had a parallel with the giving of the covenant. Both covenant and sacrifice acted to bind the people together with Yahweh their God. In fact, a sacrifice often accompanied the covenant-making process as a sign of blessing. This sign pointed to the fellowship and relationship that the covenant had fostered. Sacrifice in this context was not offered to appease or to win favour. It was more of a thank offering expressing gratitude to God for his generosity. It marked a deepening of fellowship whereby the people could identify themselves afresh with God's cause and his laws.

Repentance for wrongs committed

Clearly, a major intent of sacrifice was related to its function as a sin offering designed to address the sin of an individual or even a nation. It would be a mistake to think that such actions were merely primitive and foolish attempts to appease God or the gods. This was not an attempt to buy off God with the monetary value of the gift. Clearly the people of Israel never thought of God as one who could be manipulated in this kind of way. That approach could only lead back to a paganism already rejected by Israel. What then was the point of such a sacrifice?

There are at least three elements in the offering of a sin sacrifice. First, there is the requirement of a repentant attitude. Those who were making the offering were expected to be contrite. This is not a refusal to take wrongdoing seriously by simply removing the effects of sin with a gift – buying favour. Rather, it demonstrates an acceptance of blame and a determination to renew the relationship which has been broken by the penitent's wrong action.

At a very simple level, if my wife and I have argued and I want to say 'sorry', I might very well buy some flowers. Now I don't for a minute think that I can buy my wife's favour for the price of some flowers, not even very expensive red roses. Nor would I think very highly of her if I could. But if reconciliation is to take place, the gift might act as an indicator of my readiness to apologise and begin again.

Second, making a sin offering is a public event. It involves the help of others, probably a priest, and it takes place in a setting which indicates that there is a social dimension to this event. In other words this is not a matter of simply saying 'sorry' and then quickly moving on. There is a recognition that sin has public and not merely private consequences. The action of making sin and repentance public is to indicate that this is a serious offence which is being addressed in a similarly serious manner. In medieval Europe even kings were expected to engage in public penance when appropriate. The tradition exercised by the sovereign of England in the giving of the Maundy money echoes this ancient tradition. Today, wise politicians have learnt that it can be important to acknowledge wrongdoing and to apologise quickly even if the setting is the press conference rather than the cathedral.

Third, particularly in the case of Israel, a sin offering was also seen as a requirement laid down by God. In that sense sacrifices could not be avoided. They were an essential part of the renewing of the relationship with God. While at one level the requirements of God are not amenable to negotiation, it hardly takes much imagination to see that sacrifices were not so much a sign of the hardness and wrath of God as they were an indicator of his mercy and love.

To offer a means of rebuilding relationships with God not only reveals the consistent kindness of God, given the equally consistent failure of humanity, it also demonstrated that God took evil seriously. Wrongdoing does matter, not just in terms of the relationship with the creator but also in the realm of human affairs. In modelling the nature of true relationship, the God of Israel was also offering a basis for good human relationships both in family life but also in society more widely. In short, wrongdoing that leads to broken relationships is serious and needs to be addressed with true penitence leading to full forgiveness.

The place of the cross

In view of all that has been written so far in this chapter, it might be tempting to conclude that the system that was in place prior to the coming of Jesus was completely adequate. Sin was taken seriously and a means of dealing with that sin was clearly available. It all connected with the human needs already expressed in older more primal religions. What more was really needed?

As we will see in later chapters, part of the significance of the cross lay in who was being crucified. For the moment it is only necessary to comment that the sacrifice of Jesus on the cross was farther reaching in its effect than any sacrifice that it was replacing. This was so in a number of important ways.

First, as we saw in chapter 1, the book of Hebrews points out that the sacrifice of bulls and other animals in the worship of the temple addressed the immediate reality of sin in terms of its personal and social consequences. This was good in that God had instituted such an arrangement to deal with the effects of sin which allowed people to have fresh starts in their lives. However, these sacrifices never attempted to deal with the underlying cause or condition of sin itself. By contrast, the cross offered a much more radical and comprehensive grappling with the sin question.

Second, the reason why the cross had this effect is best illustrated by remembering that whereas the normal sacrifice in the temple dealt with the sins of individuals, the cross was attempting to meet sin at a cosmic level. The sin that was being confronted was not just the sin of individual humans but a much more significant cosmic rebellion of which human sinning was merely a part. The Scriptures inform us that Lucifer and those angels which had followed him had rebelled against God and by means of the temptation worked out in the fall had enmeshed humanity in that rebellion. Lucifer's attempt was to replace God.

For the purposes of our discussion it does not matter whether you believe in a literal Lucifer, a literal rebellion and a literal fall. Another way of expressing the same meaning contained in the biblical account of the fall is to suggest that in opting to create a moral universe God offered the possibility of saying 'no' to himself. This 'no' possibility was always likely to be accepted by humanity but also by the whole created order. An embrace of a 'no' to God rather than accepting his 'yes' to us is where the whole problem of sin begins. The reality of sin can be expressed either as rebellion or as alienation. Christ's action on the cross represents the very first absolute 'yes' to God that the creation has witnessed. It was Christ's unconditional 'yes' to God that brought about the undoing of evil.

That might be well and good for Jesus, and indeed if such a thing is true it does begin to become clear how it is that neither evil nor death itself could exercise any claim over him. But what has that to do with us? This is where we need to turn to the language of substitution. Christ died for us on the cross, not just in our place or even on our behalf, though both these suggestions are true. More particularly, his death on a cross represented an inclusive act. His identification with our human plight, together with his 'yes' to God allows us to be embraced by that same 'yes'. Christ did for us what we could never do for ourselves. He takes us with him as we offer a 'yes' to Christ.

Third, the action of Christ transcends the religious and cultural dimension represented by Israel or the Jewish people. His action on a cross allowed the essentials of the revelation of God in the Old Testament to be transmitted to every culture and so to every people in the world. The cross is a universal event which no single culture ever fully comprehends. Indeed the cross acts as an event outside even the Jewish and Graeco-Roman cultures in which it was originally set. It was a scandal to the Jews and foolishness to the Greeks. The cross both judges all cultures and in doing so simultaneously offers them a saving hope. By embracing the 'yes' of Christ uttered from the cross, all cultures can be affirmed in their implicit 'yes' to God and challenged to change in their implicit 'no' to God.

Fourth, the sacrifice of Christ on the cross was the means of establishing the new covenant with God which replaced the old covenant made on behalf of Israel by Moses. As we have seen, the old covenant had a number of inadequacies. It was limited to the Jewish people and required both the context of the promised land and the worship of the temple to operate. Perhaps most seriously of all, its conditions had been ignored so many times by the people of Israel that the prophets of Israel began to look for a time when there would be a new covenant written on the hearts of the people. This new covenant would not be limited to a single racial and religious inheritance but would be open to all those who would have faith. The sacrifice of Jesus as the paschal lamb established this new covenant.

This element of Christ's sacrifice that atones for our sins picks up Paul's images of propitiation and redemption. A price is paid by Christ for our freedom to obtain release from the bondage of sin. That freedom is legitimately paid for by the death of Christ because his complete 'yes' to God was willing to take him even to the point of a suffering death. That was the place towards which evil always pushed him and the one place where evil in its 'no' to God would never be willing to go. The blood offering of Christ expiates or blots out our sins. We are enabled through faith and repentance to grasp hold of Christ's 'yes' towards God. To go with him where we could otherwise never go. His offering of himself becomes our offering of ourselves as we turn towards the promise contained in the cross. Our basic desire to utter 'yes' to Christ allows us to be reconciled to God because of the cross. The meaning and content of that reconciliation is the subject of the next chapter.

Questions

1. Can it be right to die in the place of others? Do we have the right to make such a sacrifice and what do we make of those who act in such a way?
2. Can you think of experiences that you have had which have led to a sense of 'wonder' about life?
3. What actions do we personally engage in to demonstrate our gratitude to God for the gift of life?
4. If you wanted someone to forgive you for something you had done, where would you begin? Can you think of examples in your own life where forgiveness has been a necessary and helpful experience?
5. What does the cross tell us about the importance of who it was that was crucified on the cross? Would any well-intentioned death have done as much as the death of Jesus and if not, why not?

Notes

1. This story is told by Victor Gollancz in his book, *A Year of Grace*, Victor Gollancz, London, 1950, pp.207–209.
2. Church of England Newspaper, 9 August 1991, p.16, Article by Michael Marshall.

5

The Reconciling Cross

This chapter looks at the key issues of sin, freedom, justice, suffering and forgiveness. What do these terms mean and how do they relate to each other?

The Reconciling Cross

I listened to her story with a fascination that wanted to interrupt, to question, to offer support. But the story itself demanded silence. In some ways the ingredients were unremarkable. It was the story of a single mother who had given up her twin babies for adoption. Since then she had married and had more children. After a full thirty years she received the one phone call that she had always wondered over. Her daughters wanted to get in touch. For more than half an hour I listened to this very human story of pain and joy, of explanations, of catching up with lost lives. Reconciliation is wonderful but it is costly.

A very similar set of dilemmas is presented in the film *Sex and Lies*. Some critics have suggested that most of the film is an extended prologue leading to the ten-minute section when all of the facts tumble out and uncomfortable realities are faced. The first part of the film consists of an almost maddeningly long explanation of the complexity of the situation. And that is often the reality, the human circumstances and actions that lead to the construction of painful situations are usually extraordinarily complex and difficult to unravel. That is also part of the story of reconciliation.

Sorting out the sin question

Painful and destructive as these situations might be, we wouldn't normally think of using the word 'sin' to describe them. Is that simply because the world has changed? Is it merely the case that our moral framework has shifted so that the word 'sin' is no longer in fashion? Would it be better simply to describe the sexual activity that produced these complex situations as sin and be done with it? Curiously, it is often those who do not know the Bible well who imagine that it is a textbook of legal denunciation, always ready with the quick word of condemnation. The reality is more complex.

The Bible speaks of sin in at least three kinds of ways. First, sin is a state of being, essentially an alienation from God. Sin in this sense is not merely negative, that is to say, an absence of communion with God. It has a more malevolent and active character than that. Paul speaks of sin as a force that has the power to enslave and even overpower us. In Romans we read: 'So I find this law at work. When I want to do good, evil is right there with me. For in my inner being I delight in God's law, but I see another law at work in the members of my body, waging war against the law of my mind and making me a prisoner of the law of sin at work within my members' (Romans 7:21–23). The kind of sin that Paul is referring to seems to be external to humanity but nevertheless it is able to exert a deceptive influence on human life. For Paul there is an essential conflict between the law of sin and the law of life.

Second, the Bible speaks of sin in terms of the breaking

of relationship or covenant. From the perspective of the Hebrew mind, all life is upheld by covenant, whether with God or with one's neighbour or even in the context of a landlord-tenant relationship. There is an agreement that is in force in which due honour is given to both participants. Sin is the breaking of that covenant such that the relationship is fractured. That same sin produces a disharmony in stark contrast to the harmony that a covenant relationship upholds. Sin of this kind involves rebellion or overturning of that which is good.

Third, there is the notion of sin which is more deeply rooted in an individual's life. This understanding of sin has to do with the fundamental attitude of the individual towards God, towards the upholding of that which is good (the covenant), and towards his or her neighbours. A refusal to lean towards goodness indicates a kind of disease of the soul which requires a drastic remedy. Such a person may be a victim or they may be acting of their own volition but the effect is the same. What matters here is not the particular actions of the individual but the state from which they flow. Bob Dylan conveys something of that meaning in his description of a prostitute in his song 'Desolation Row': 'Her profession's her religion, her sin is her lifelessness. Although her eyes are fixed upon, Noah's great rainbow, she spends her time peeking, into Desolation Row.'[1] The hope of the covenant (the rainbow) is replaced by the possibility and indeed likelihood of hopeless destruction (Desolation Row).

Many of the situations in which we find ourselves are not simply the consequence of our own foolish actions, even if that is sometimes the case. More often than not, sin in all three of its meanings has been at work. We have been the subject of forces that operate beyond us. We have a dulled conscience that does not recognise the lifelessness towards which we lean. These unpromising realities are compounded by our willing co-operation, whether by ignorance or by deliberate foolishness, to act in ways that cause relationships to be broken.

Freedom and forgiveness

Three immediate questions flow from a recognition of the reality of sin. First, who is to blame? The most complex answer of the Bible is to suggest that there is a cosmic conflict in which we are all inevitably caught up. That conflict can be personified by saying, 'It is the fault of Lucifer.' Such an excuse is not as facile as it may sound. There are many in this world who are themselves such victims of violence and terror that their appalling actions can be understood to a considerable degree. The child soldiers of Africa, brutalised from an early age and taught to murder can hardly be held entirely responsible for their own actions.

Yet, even in these extreme cases, the Bible also wants to say that none of us are so far removed from the divine spark involved in our creation that all sense of wrong-doing is removed. Whatever the extenuating circumstances, some responsibility for our actions remains.

That brings us to the second question, how can individuals allow themselves to be caught in a rebellion which leads to such lifelessness? The Bible suggests that we have a foolish tendency to prefer evil to good: 'This is the verdict: Light has come into the world, but men loved darkness instead of light because their deeds were evil' (John 3:19). There is a strange perversity which causes otherwise intelligent people to argue for that which leads to destruction. Jacques Ellul wonders at the foolishness of the intelligent:

The human wickedness that tends spontaneously to respect nothing coincides with the collective imbecility of the race. The same people who can be refined and intelligent and cultivated become imbeciles when they are caught up in mass movements: Heidegger and Nazism, Sartre and Stalinist communism, and how many others. I watch hundreds of people plunge into absurd and wicked causes.[2]

The key phrase used by Ellul concerns the respect for nothing. This involves a profound misunderstanding of the nature of freedom. The idea that humankind is autonomous and so free of any need to consider the existence of God, usually leads tragically to an abuse of the very freedom that is so energetically proclaimed. The thinker Lesslie Newbigin liked to use the analogy of children playing in a park. Around the park are large railings. These boundary fences are there to prevent the children from harm. They have the useful function of stopping children running into a busy road. Are we to conclude that the railings are erected to enhance the freedom of safe play or to rob children of an unfettered freedom of movement? The laws of God are intended to add to our safety not to remove our freedom.

In a perverse way the very grasping of a freedom which is concerned only for the rights of individuals and never for our responsibilities under covenant leads only to the undermining of freedom. To seek the freedom to do whatever we want without any regard for the consequences tends to lead to the loss of freedom.

The third question inevitably asks, 'Is there a solution to the situation in which we find ourselves?' Can our abuse of freedom be countermanded in such a way that we might find true freedom? Can our natural involvement in processes of rebellion which are far greater than our individual existences ever be transcended? Can we ever hope to live in true, life-giving covenant with God, our neighbours and those in our own families? Can we escape that which has enmeshed us?

It is at this point that we have to come to terms with the fact that freedom can only be restored if forgiveness is exercised. Such a far-reaching claim requires some further examination. The current popularity of television confessional chat shows is revealing. From the more lurid Springer-type shows through to those programmes with a stronger counselling element, there is a consistent attempt to bring a degree of reconciliation to various broken relationships. Apparent success in coming closer, in healing painful or damaged relationships is usually greeted with loud applause by the audience. Reconciliation is the desired outcome.

It doesn't take long to see that no progress is made in solving the hurts of the past without at least an acknowledgement of past hurts, a willingness to say sorry, and a commitment to act differently in the future. Nor can the word 'sorry' simply be an insincere device. For healing to happen there must be a perception that the sorrow expressed carries conviction. Only when reconciliation has been effected, presumably after the actual television show, can there be a possibility of a new start in the relationship which would involve the rebuilding of trust and so the reintroduction of creative freedom in the relationship. The process of reconciliation requires the presence of forgiveness and repentance.

There seems to be a natural tendency to resist our need for any kind of repentance or forgiveness. Why can't God, or whoever else we have offended, simply overlook all that has happened without the need for forgiveness and repentance?

The problem with forgiveness is that we seem to know intuitively that forgiveness and repentance is a costly process.

In the summer of 1998 the England football team lost a key World Cup match on penalties. They were out of the Cup. It was difficult for many to forget that they had played much of the match with just ten men. The missing man, David Beckham, had been sent off for a foolish foul. Many in the nation and certainly in the media took the easy view that the team might have won if only Beckham had not acted so irresponsibly. There was something of a furore in the press. In the midst of this controversy, the England manager, Glen Hoddle, asked people to forgive Beckham, to give him another chance.

The Bible Society decided to pick up this remark and encourage people to respond to the challenge of forgiveness. A press release along these lines was issued. At first there was little or no response, and then, around a week after the initial release, it was as if the floodgates opened. *The Daily Telegraph* carried the item on the front page and then breakfast television picked it up. From then on other national media joined in together with numerous local radio stations and even the BBC world service and Sky TV asking for interviews. It felt for a few days like a media feeding frenzy. One local radio station carried out a poll of its listeners and a very high percentage, certainly a majority, of listeners were not prepared to forgive Beckham. What was this all about? Why would people steadfastly refuse to forgive someone who had never injured them personally?

The answer seemed to lie in the fact that it was easier to have a scapegoat, someone who could be blamed, someone else who could carry the weight of defeat at the hands of an old enemy. To forgive Beckham was somehow to bear the cost of the defeat oneself. It was as if the pain felt by each fan could somehow be ameliorated by placing the blame firmly at the feet, quite literally, of someone else. To forgive, even in this relatively trivial and distant case, carried a cost and the preference was to ask someone else to pay it.

Justice cries out for an answer

So far we have looked at the need for forgiveness and repentance to be present in the process of forgiveness. Even if we are not prepared to forgive, then someone (at times one might feel anyone) is required to pay a price. But why should that be? Why is it necessary for a price to be paid? That brings us to an inescapable and deeply uncomfortable reality. Doesn't the act of forgiving simply remove the need for any penalty to be paid?

Where wrong has been done, where injustice has been committed, justice calls out for an answer. Not simply the consequences of wrongdoing, but the wrong itself calls out for some recompense. Can there be said to be any justice if God is not just? In the face of many wrongs, in the midst of profound evil, isn't it the business of God to be talking of justice, of punishment, even of vengeance for the wronged rather than think of repentance, forgiveness and reconciliation?

The desire for just deserts to be meted out to those who commit crime is an ancient theme. The thirst for retribution runs deep. In primitive times it was possible for blood feuds to run sufficiently deep that whole tribes could be murdered. In more recent times, we can see in contemporary history that the longing for revenge is remarkably close to the actuality of genocide. The judicial system is in part an attempt to ensure that revenge does not run in unbridled fashion, destroying all who stand in its path. Legal codes attempt to apply punishments which are at least commensurate with the wrong that has been committed. They represent an attempt at fairness so that society can be ordered and stable. The exercise of a sound system of justice is felt to be an essential ingredient in a healthy society.

But those who are familiar with any judicial system will know that what seems to be common sense actually comes replete with difficulty. The two major theories of justice revolve around the themes of utilitarianism and retributivism. The utilitarian theme emphasises the practical outcomes of justice. Proper punishment should produce a deterrent effect such that society is protected from the worst excesses of crime. Sentencing is intended to ensure that the individual criminal is set on the path to reform. In other words, the apparent 'harm' of punishment is offset by the 'good' practical consequences for society. The needs of the individual who has been wronged are seen as less important than the good of the greater society and utilitarian justice has that greater good as its major focus. It doesn't take much awareness of the effect of prisons to realise that utilitarian theory quickly founders on the simple fact that prison usually fails to reform and arguably acts as a university of crime. The greater good fails to materialise and so the argument for any kind of punishment falters.

The retributivist theory centres around the idea that criminals must simply pay for their crime. In short, punishment is intrinsically moral and just. This theory pays more attention to the individual who has been wronged. It is felt that the pain and loss of the victim can only be ameliorated if punishment is handed out. The difficulty in such a moral stand lies precisely in the moral dilemma associated with knowing when proper or appropriate punishment has been delivered. In such a system it is difficult to take account of extenuating circumstances. A single code is too inflexible to be entirely appropriate in every situation. As one writer has suggested: 'Acting justly in the retributivist sense therefore becomes a near impossibility, for as Hegel pointed out, "Injustice is done at once if there is one lash too many, or one dollar, one cent, one week in prison, or one day, too many or too few."'[3]

True justice is therefore a much more personal matter. Arguably it involves relationships and not just an arbitrary code. The introduction of a personal element means that justice can be tempered with mercy. But before mercy can even enter the stage, it has to be faced that wrongdoing has consequences for both victim and perpetrator. Justice insists that those consequences cannot simply be brushed aside. It follows therefore that the one who forgives, who exercises mercy, carries some or all of the consequences of the crime. In very simple terms, if someone deliberately breaks my window and I catch that person and then decide to exercise forgiveness, then it necessarily follows that I am prepared to pay for the cost of repairing the window. The important point is that the window has been broken, it cannot be repaired without a cost to someone. Usually, the one who forgives is prepared to bear the cost of the wrong.

In much more complex terms, we can see how this very basic principle is outworked in cases where murder has been committed. One of the very moving outcomes of the conflict in Northern Ireland has been to witness those occasions when individuals have lost loved ones and have insisted on offering forgiveness to those who committed the murder. The offer of forgiveness does not come without a price but the price is borne by the ones with the strength and capacity, the moral courage, to forgive. It is the Christian claim that the realities of justice, mercy, forgiveness, repentance and the establishment of personal involvement are all brought together by the reconciling event of the cross. Something of the same process has been witnessed in the various attempts to bring healing in the post-apartheid situation in South Africa.

The God who suffers

In a lecture on mission,[4] the notable South African academic, David Bosch, drew attention to a novel by the Japanese author Shusaku Endo.[5] The novel tells the story of a Jesuit priest, Father Rodrigues. The background to the book concerns the growth and then the persecution of the Christian community in the early seventeenth century. It is not necessarily well known that one of the earliest Jesuit priests, Francis Xavier, visited Japan in 1549. He was well received and his missionary work flourished, so much so that within a single generation a community of 150,000 Japanese Christians had come into being.

It is said that a chance remark by a Dutch sea captain caused the Japanese authorities to re-assess their view of the Christian community. In essence, the captain suggested that the missionary work of the Jesuits represented a 'softening up' phase which would be followed by full-scale colonisation either by the Portuguese or by Spain. The captain could certainly quote chapter and verse from other parts of the world where such a pattern had become apparent. Whether this comment was the only cause or not, a horrific persecution began shortly after the expulsion of all missionaries in 1614. Some missionaries were able to go underground before they were expelled in order to continue their work of encouraging the beleaguered Christian community.

The persecution was extraordinarily savage. Many Christians were executed while some were given the opportunity to renounce their faith. The Japanese persecutors were particularly anxious to force missionaries to apostatise, recognising that this would be the most effective means of rooting out Christianity altogether. They were required to trample on a bronze image of the face of Christ (a fumie) as a sign that they had recanted their faith. The torture usually consisted of being suspended upside down in a pit filled with excrement and other filth. After sixteen years, one missionary, the leader of the Japanese mission, Christovao Ferreira finally apostatised.

The novel centres on the experiences of Ferreira's replacement, Father Sebastian Rodrigues, especially following his capture and torture. Rodrigues did not apostatise for many months. The climax of the novel comes with the astonishing declaration of the interpreter who suddenly said to Rodrigues, 'Tonight you will certainly apostatise.' As it turns out, the interpreter was right but the means by which Rodrigues was persuaded to renounce his faith holds the secret to the message of the book. The key to the interpreter's confidence lay in his introduction of the apostate Ferreira. As Rodrigues and Ferreira talked about the moment when he apostatised, it became clear that the issue concerned the silence of God in the face of the suffering of so many who wished to follow him. The novel had the title *Silence*.

The awful truth of the silence of God then dawned on Rodrigues. It transpired that he could hear the moans of those who were being tortured. He wondered why they did not renounce their faith and was told that all of those who were being tortured had indeed recanted many times. But they would never be set free from torture until he, Rodrigues, apostatised. It was his actions that would determine the future of these suffering peasants. God seemed to be completely absent from the scene. Bosch describes the final conclusion of the novel:

> It was this silence of God that has given Endo's novel its title – the silence of a God, a Christ, who did not respond to prayers or to torture. Still, in the end the silence was broken. Christ did speak to Rodrigues – not, however, the beautiful, haloed, and serene Christ of devotions, but the Christ of the twisted and dented *fumie*, the Christ whose face had been distorted by many feet, the concave, ugly Christ, the trampled-upon and suffering Christ. And what this Christ was saying to the priest shocked him to the marrow, 'Trample, trample! . . . It was to be trampled on by men that I was born into this world. It was to share men's pain that I carried my cross.' And the novelist writes: 'The priest placed his foot on the *fumie*. Dawn broke. And in the far distance the cock crew.'[6]

The cross reveals to us, not the silence of a God who does not care, but the silence of a God who cares so much that he offers no word of self defence to save himself from the torture of execution on the cross. Then, and ever since he has given himself to humanity, to be despised and rejected. He has himself borne the cost of all of the sinfulness of humanity and it is precisely because he has not asked anyone else to pay the price of sin but has taken it upon himself, that he is able to offer forgiveness from the cross.

That offer of forgiveness never downplays the seriousness of sin and the importance of justice. Not only does the cross meet the reasonable demands of justice – the price of wrongdoing is paid – but it also takes sin seriously at another level. The aim of the cross is reconciliation and the offer of forgiveness is certainly the most crucial element in the process of reconciliation. But it is not just a remote action that bears no relationship to the response of humankind. The reconciling act of God stands in principle for all people in all times but it does require a personal response to make God's action effective. The gift of forgiveness is permanently on offer but it can never become ours until we accept it and so make it our own. It is at the cross that the apparently conflicting demands of justice, forgiveness, mercy, repentance and reconciliation meet. In Endo's novel the debate with God went on after his suffering had ended: 'Long after the terrible ordeal he had gone through, Fr Rodrigues was arguing bitterly with Christ, saying to him, "Lord, I resented your silence," to which Christ replied, "I was not silent. I suffered beside you."'[7]

Questions

1. What do you understand by the term 'sin'?
2. Why can't God merely overlook our wrongdoing without the need for any specific remedy?
3. Does the need for justice mean that forgiveness is ever a bad idea?
4. What do we make of the 'silence of God' described in this chapter?
5. Does God forgive us whether or not we ask for forgiveness?

Notes

1. 'Desolation Row' can be found on the albums *Highway 61 Revisited* and *Unplugged*, both by Bob Dylan.
2. Jacques Ellul, *What I Believe*, William Eerdmans Publishing Co, Michigan, USA, 1989, pp.63ff.

3. Michael Schluter, *The 'R' Factor*, Hodder & Stoughton, London, 1993, p.259.
4. David Bosch. The lecture is published as a booklet by the Selly Oak Colleges under the title *The Vulnerability of Mission*, Birmingham, 1991.
5. *The Vulnerability of Mission*, pp.1f.
6. *Ibid.*, p.2.
7. *Ibid.*, p.5.

6

It is for Freedom that Christ has Set Us Free

This chapter takes up the theme of freedom in more detail
and relates it to the question of the love of God. It specifically explores the nature of the freedom to which the cross
directs us and shows how God's love is expressed through
the cross. It concludes by asking what our proper response
to the love of God might be.

It is for Freedom that Christ has Set Us Free

Freedom is a much-used word and for many in the twentieth century has been a rare commodity. When freedom comes to those who have been deprived of liberty, their reactions are usually rather diverse. Over the last few years we have become accustomed in the UK to watching the release of prisoners whose sentences have been overturned by the courts as 'unsafe verdicts'. Television cameras are always present to witness the moment of release. The immediate emotional responses of the prisoners together with their relatives and friends range from anger at the wrong done, relief that it is all over, through to an unbridled joy as the exhilarating prospect of living in freedom takes hold.

Television cameras also recorded the astonishing moments when the growing crowds in the former East Germany sensed that their moment had come. The genesis of a movement for freedom had formed as a simple prayer meeting in a Lutheran church in Leipzig. The prayer meetings had become vigils and then candlelit marches. The sense of confidence grew and spread until eventually the people stood on top of the symbol of their imprisonment, the Berlin Wall itself, and piece by piece tore it down.

The raw human emotion of those hours made for great television but it was much more than dramatic footage. Those in the West who watched were struck with a sense of amazement. Few had ever imagined that such scenes would ever be witnessed. There was an astonishing power in the graphic presentation of a mass grasping of freedom.

In the case of those who had been wrongly imprisoned, the Guildford five and the Birmingham six, as well as in the case of the population of East Germany, these were people whose freedom was deserved and proper. Yet even in the case of those who have accepted guilt but who have been offered pardon, the wonder at the dawning of freedom is no less real.

It could be argued that sometimes our interest might be rather voyeuristic. The South Koreans released a North Korean prisoner during the early part of 1999 as part of an amnesty programme. The press was fascinated by the fact that the prisoner in question had been in solitary confinement for forty years. Inevitably the media wanted to ask the questions that were in the minds of many: 'How had he survived such an ordeal?', 'What had motivated him to keep going?', 'How can any cause warrant such loyalty?', 'How would he cope with a world that was now entirely different from that which he had known as a much younger man?' But even apart from these slightly trivial questions, it is hard to deny the underlying sense of pleasure that mercy had been shown. Freedom has its own intrinsic allure.

The quest for freedom extends to all those who have felt oppressed and not just to those who are physically incarcerated. It is hard to forget the action, marches and speeches of Martin Luther King. One of his well-known speeches included the memorable passage, 'Free at last, free at last. Thank God Almighty, we are free at last.' What did King mean by such a statement? At a very basic level, he was quoting the words of a Negro spiritual and looking forward to a time that could come. In the immediate context in which he found himself, he had not won any particular victory in terms of the passing of legislation. Certainly his marches, including the one in Washington that he was addressing that day, were attracting attention.[1] Many have speculated as to what he did precisely mean but he seemed to be referring to something much more profound than campaign successes. It was as if his own commitment to a cause had brought him, emotionally, spiritually, psychologically, to a point where he had gained his own internal freedom. He had somehow glimpsed the future and in so doing was able to live in that future as if it were a current reality. He had become personally free of all the hate directed at him, the fear that he might not succeed, the worry of the practical campaign. All that had gone as he grasped hold of his own sense of personal liberty.

Martin Luther King's expression of freedom was close in its own way to the sentiments expressed by an actual prisoner, Terry Waite. Broadcasting on the BBC, Terry Waite reflected on his years of imprisonment by terrorists in Lebanon. He remembered that he had told his captives, 'You can take possession of my body and of my mind, and you have already done so, but you can never take possession of my soul. That is not yours to possess.'[2]

Terry Waite had grasped something of tremendous importance in relation to the nature of freedom. Being free is not in the first instance to do with personal physical liberty, much though we all insist on its importance. True freedom is related to a spiritual quest regardless of our physical surroundings. Those who are physically at liberty and those who are wealthy materially still find themselves yearning for something more, for a freedom from that which inwardly oppresses. Such a quest is the goal of all of the major world religions and it is directly addressed by the event of the cross.

As we saw in Chapter 3, the term 'justification' came originally from the world of the law. It emphasises that aspect of the cross which is related to release from sentence, of being set free. But however much we might rejoice in the notion of freedom, the problem for late twentieth- century/ early twenty-first century Westerners, lies in understanding the nature of the sentence from which we have been set free. If we cannot understand the sentence, and indeed if we suspect that the very sentence itself is unjust then we certainly cannot understand the value of the pardon.

Indeed, we can even distort the nature of the gift of God because the freedom we speak of sounds more like freedom from an unjust sentence, from oppressive guilt. In such a scenario the cross is just more religious jargon. We can easily convince ourselves that the real problem is religion itself and the guilt it places on us. The culprit who stands in the dock is God himself and we are the wronged and innocent party claiming our own rightful freedom from the harm of enforced guilt. So, given the difficulty we have in understanding the problem from which we have been set free, is there a way ahead?

The disease of the soul

Let us remind ourselves that the sentence from which Christ on the cross sets us free is not a sentence imposed by God because we have somehow failed to carry out his wishes. The sentence is imposed by the nature of sin itself. Certainly there are particular sins, which flow from the fundamental condition of sin, and it is certainly true that God also forgives these sins. But the core problem is not our annoying habit of doing wrong so much as the underlying condition that plagues the human soul. We might call that condition the disease of the soul. It is that disease that produces ingrained habits so deep that they amount to a kind of slavery.

At its most basic level sin constitutes a decision to live without reference to God. This has even been presented by philosophers as the ultimate enlightenment, as a throwing off of the childish need for any kind of dependence upon God. We claim for ourselves autonomy as free individuals, unfettered by superstition or religious claptrap.

Yet the sad experience of humanity reveals that such claims lead us ever more profoundly into absurdity and unhappiness. We experience an acute sense of lost-ness. Writers express that feeling of angst in many ways. Some speak of a profound loneliness, others of an identity crisis, still others of longing for some kind of home. The Catholic writer Henri Nouwen has identified a deep yearning in secular men and women for a sense of being loved – of needing to know that one is the beloved of God.

Why should it be so hard to accept that we are the beloved – unconditionally loved by God? Two key areas of self-doubt are clear to the mystics of old. The first is the awareness that we hear many negative voices in our lives all of which raise many doubts for us. It may be a teacher or even a parent – those charged with raising our self-esteem – who have acted towards us in such a way that our confidence, our proper sense of self-esteem has been fatally wounded. But even if this is not the case, even if we have been surrounded by those who tenderly love and care for us, there remains the second and more troubling voice – that of our own dark side, accusing and admonishing us.

Few of us discover much about our dark side until the second half of our life, not because the dark side of our existence is not present throughout our lives but simply because it requires some maturity to face it. Another way of speaking about our dark side is to think of it as our shadow side. The shadow side of who we are is genuinely part of us but it is a part of who we are that we generally do not like to know about. Yet without facing our dark side we cannot know who we are and what we might become. Henri Nouwen identifies the uncomfortable question that comes to us from the shadow side of our life:

> Beneath all my seemingly strong self-confidence there remained the question; 'If all those who shower me with so much attention could see me and know me in my innermost self, would they still love me?' That agonizing question, rooted in my inner shadow, kept persecuting me and made me run away from the very place where that quiet voice calling me the Beloved could be heard.[3]

The questions that flow from our own conscious self-doubt and from our deeper shadow side reflect our profound awareness that all is not well with our soul. For some people, such self-knowledge is simply avoided, denied and suppressed. But for most people these issues arise at some point in life even if they are not the common currency of everyday conversation.[4] Our desire to address these questions leads to a quest to cure the disease of our souls whether or not we think of it in precisely these terms. In pursuing such a spiritual journey two very different false trails wait to entrap us.

Cheap grace

The theologian and church leader, Dietrich Bonhoeffer was the first to popularise the phrase 'cheap grace'. He had in mind the specific situation of Nazi Germany in the 1930s. Bonhoeffer's own convictions led to him to become involved in a bomb plot designed to assassinate Hitler. The attempt failed and Bonhoeffer was executed in a concentration camp during the Second World War. But the notion of 'cheap grace' has certainly not been confined to the time of Bonhoeffer. The term describes any view of the Christian faith which seems to accept the apparent benefits of the Christian life, for example, the forgiveness of sins and life everlasting, without making any demands on human behaviour.

The writer Dallas Willard, commenting on the current Christian scene in the United States describes 'cheap grace' in these terms:

> It says that you can have a faith in Christ that brings forgiveness, while in every other respect your life is no different from that of others who have no faith in Christ at all. This view so pleasingly presented on bumpers and trinkets has deep historical roots. It is by now worked out in many sober tomes of theology, lived out by multitudes of those who sincerely self-identify as Christians.[5]

How could anyone imagine that such a way of living could possibly do justice to the death of Christ on a cross? How could anyone think that such a travesty of Christian living could possibly square with the teachings and example of Jesus? The answer has a great deal to do with a twisted understanding of the doctrine of justification. Two crucial misunderstandings lay the foundation for this kind of 'cheap grace'.

The first misunderstanding is to identify the Christian faith as entirely and only concerned with the forgiveness of sins. It is as if the birth of Jesus took place only in order for him to die on a cross with all that took place between these two events acting as incidental time-fillers or at best as an illuminating precursor designed to explain the meaning of the cross. Such thinking tends to view the Christian faith in consumerist terms. The great perceived consumer benefit is that of a blanket forgiveness, unrelated to personal behaviour, which leads to peace of mind in this life and an assured eternal destiny in the next. There are no moral quandaries in such a system. A good God is only concerned to forgive, to accept sinners, to offer blessing, to bring a sense of spiritual well-being. He asks nothing in return beyond a willingness to accept such blessing. Who would not want to sign up for 'free gifts' on this kind of cosmic scale?

The second misunderstanding relates to the idea that the action of Christ on the cross leads to a kind of justification which is only dependent on the action of God and has nothing at all to do with human response. It is as if the recipients of this astonishing generosity are only passive patients unable to refuse the dosage of grace administered by God. Of course it is true that the initiative does belong with God and that the justification accomplished on the cross is external to humankind. But to reduce the action of God to a mechanical formula unrelated to the heart of human beings is to make a travesty of the work of Christ.

The combination of these two errors leads to a Christianity in which personal morality is unrelated to Christian commitment. There comes a disconnection between lifestyle and Christian belief. The escape clause centres on the certain knowledge that none of us are perfect and the forgiveness of God covers this inescapable reality. The failure of so many Christian leaders in the United States to live exemplary lifestyles has led to a huge degree of scepticism concerning the integrity of the Church. It has almost come to the point where high profile leaders are assumed to be hypocrites. It is not a question of whether they have significant skeletons in the cupboard so much as how adept they might be at hiding them.

Nor is such pessimism confined to leaders. Social studies have concluded that church attendance no longer acts as a predicator of personal behaviour except in a negative sense. One study has suggested that those who attend church in America are now more likely to have their marriages end in divorce, not less likely. The offer of forgiveness from God seems to serve to diminish the personal pain and social stigma of divorce. But does God really seek to relate to us in such a way? Most of Christian history would cry out, 'No, not at all.'

Winning God's favour

It is clear that an undue emphasis on the free offer of grace can lead to a devalued 'cheap grace'. But there is an opposite danger. In very simple terms it can be characterised as an attempt to win the favour of God, in short to earn one's salvation. Put in such stark terms, few would seriously believe that it is possible to persuade God to accept us on the basis of our good deeds. But the proposition is rarely put so simply. In reality, the notion that our deeds will be important in persuading God to accept us is psychologically attractive.

The attempt to win God's favour comes in different

forms. Those who have been involved in Christian ministry will know how widespread this idea is among those
who either never or rarely attend church. The discovery
that you are a clergyman leads surprisingly often to a
rather one-sided conversation in which the other person
attempts to persuade you (or possibly themselves) that
despite the fact that they do not attend church their
eternal destiny is not really in doubt.

How have they reached this conclusion? Basically
because they believe themselves to be 'a good person'.
What is the evidence? They help people, they pray from
time to time and although they may have committed
minor sins (occasional white lies and small-scale theft
from one's employer), these are the things that everybody
does. After all, no one is perfect (including those who
attend church), and they have never really done anyone
any harm. So, taking all these things into consideration it
would seem that on balance God doesn't have enough
evidence to convict. Conclusion? On the day of judgement
I will probably be all right. I can't be certain but I think so.
Clearly they are hoping that as a clergyman you can be
counted on to confirm their view. A brief conversation
over cheese and biscuits in a crowded corner is rarely
the moment to dent such well ingrained assumptions.

If that is the popular end of such a conviction, there is a
much more adequately constructed intellectual tradition
which takes a similar position. In more recent times it can
be characterised as the social gospel. In the nineteenth
century it was more properly called 'liberal theology' and
there can be little doubt that it had an intellectual and
practical force which should not be lightly dismissed. It is
true that in the twentieth century that older liberal theology
deteriorated so that it often became only a social gospel. In

such thinking the cross becomes little more than an example of extreme commitment to a cause. The death of Christ becomes merely a rallying cry to fight against injustice. Jesus is seen primarily as a martyr for the cause of the poor and oppressed. The kingdom of God comes only to the extent that we create it. We are seen as righteous by God because of our identification with righteous causes. Such crusades can be morally exhilarating but spiritually exhausting.

In more recent times many of those who have felt themselves to be good people as well as those who have become spiritually and emotionally drained by good causes have sought to add spiritual experiences in their deeper quest for meaning and self-understanding. Such an approach to spirituality may well produce personal benefits simply as a consequence of being still rather than active, of listening rather than talking. But even this concern for some kind of spirituality carries with it the implication that there is some kind of system for earning points with God. There remains the danger that every spiritual discipline is seen as only another way of gaining access to God, of bending his favour, of accumulating credit. There is every reason for thinking that this kind of approach to spirituality ends in profound spiritual, emotional and psychological disappointment.

Bathing in the love of God

If these are the false trails waiting to mislead us, what then is the path that God intends for us, the way that the cross provides for us? The experience of Martin Luther can help us to grasp the issues. Luther lived as a monk towards the end of the Middle Ages. At this time, theological debate centred on the question of how we please God. The term justification was used as theological shorthand to mean entering into a right relationship with God. This was certainly Luther's concern and as a devout monk he had attempted every action that he could think of in order to please God.

In many ways, he could be satisfied that he was certainly a good person living a blameless life. Why then was this not enough? Why was Luther constantly left feeling that somehow he could never do enough? In part, the problem lay in his own devotion. He knew enough about God to have come to understand the holiness or the perfection of God. We might even call this the righteousness of God. Luther realised that a God who was holy and who loved justice would certainly punish sinners and therein lay the problem.

As someone who loved justice himself, Luther did not want God to take a lenient view of injustice and sin. Not for Luther the vacuous idea that God is simply obliged to welcome all 'good people' on the basis that there was not enough evidence to convict. Luther could see only too clearly that God was so holy that there were none who dared to approach him on the basis of their own good works. And that is why Luther constantly felt so inadequate. However blameless a life he led his own genuine knowledge and love of God was such that he could never feel worthy to be accepted by God.

The spiritual tension produced by this conflict was so acute that Luther began to hate God. He says, 'Far from loving that righteous God who punished sinners, I actually hated him.'[6] Eventually, the light dawned for Luther. Revelation and with it freedom, finally came. He came to the point where he was able to see that his good works could never bring him the approval of God but rather that the approval of God was already waiting for him. This was not 'cheap grace' only requiring him to passively receive.

While it was certainly true that the action was all God's and that there was nothing he could do to manufacture or create such saving faith, having accepted the gift of faith, he was now enabled to live for God. Living for God had not brought him the acceptance of God, but the acceptance of God had produced the ability to live for him.

The key phrase grasped by Luther was that 'the righteous person lives by faith'. He went on to conclude, 'This immediately made me feel as though I had been born again, and as though I had entered through open gates into paradise itself. From that moment, I saw the whole face of Scripture in a new light . . . And now, where I had once hated the phrase, "The righteousness of God", I began to love and extol it as the sweetest of phrases, so that this passage in Paul became the very gate of paradise to me.'[7]

That then is the point of the justification achieved by Christ upon the cross. In very simple terms, Christ has paid the penalty for sin and so we therefore may go free, it is just as if we had never sinned. We are forgiven but our freedom is not merely one in which the consequences of the past are avoided so much as the potential of the future is grasped. We are set free from the prison of past sin not just as miraculous escape but in order to live the life that God intends. The justification achieved by the cross has to be seen in terms of Calvary and its cost, the resurrection with its potential and Pentecost with its power. The cross propels us to a future in which our lives will be different. We are introduced to a world bathed in the love of God, a love that embraces us and a love that seeks to transform us.

Dallas Willard offers these words to express the change that God seeks in us: 'When we bring people to believe differently, they really do become different. One of the greatest weaknesses in our teaching and leadership today is that we spend so much time trying to get people to do things good people are supposed to do, without changing what they really believe.'[8]

Good works rarely bring changed beliefs so much as exhausted bodies but from changed beliefs the changed commitments of a whole life can flow. The death of Christ upon a cross is intended to introduce that different commitment, set flowing as it does from an encounter with the healing and embracing love of God. He does not just care and accept everyone in some generalised amnesty, his love extends personally, individually to us. It is the embrace of that love that allows the work of Christ upon the cross to take deep root in our lives for our good and for the good of others.

Questions

1. Is there such a thing as 'sin' that binds us or is the real problem merely a sense of guilt brought about by religion?
2. What would be the hallmarks of someone whose life had been changed by the love of God?
3. Is there any discernible difference between those who are following Jesus and those who do not claim to follow him?
4. How do we see the connection between belief and behaviour?
5. Can you think of any experiences of God that you have had which have resulted in a specific change in your life?

Notes

1. Martin Luther King's speech which contained these words was made on the occasion of the Washington March for Jobs and Freedom held on 28 August 1963.
2. *Thought for the Day*, BBC Radio 4, 1 March 1999.

3. Henri Nouwen, *Life of the Beloved*, Hodder & Stoughton, London, 1993, p.29.
4. Two people who have researched in the area of popular spirituality are Roger Edrington and David Hay. See for example Roger Edrington, *Everyday Men: Living in a Climate of Unbelief*, Peter Lang, Frankfurt, 1987, and David Hay with Rebecca Nye, *Spirit of the Child*, Fount UK, 1998.
5. Dallas Willard, *The Divine Conspiracy*, HarperCollins, London, 1998, p.44.
6. McGrath, *Luther's Theology of the Cross*, Blackwell Publishers Ltd, Oxford, 1985, p.438.
7. *Ibid.*
8. Dallas Willard, 1998, p.336.

7

Evil and the God of Love

In this chapter the reality of evil as a cosmic power is described in more detail. The significance of the cross in confronting the power of evil is explored. It suggests that the way of Jesus offers a new alternative in terms of overcoming the power of evil.

Evil and the God of Love

The painting of St John of the Cross by Salvador Dali presents an arresting and unusual visual image of the crucifixion. Christ appears on the cross seen from above. Such a perspective stands in stark contrast to the usual view in which Christ is seen from the position of an onlooker gazing upwards. Not only is Christ viewed from above but the cross seems to be suspended slightly above the sea of Galilee. The impact is to emphasise the cosmic dimensions of the cross. But the painting does not end with such an impact because the figure on the cross is clearly very human. We are invited to make a personal response in the same moment as grasping the universal themes present in the cross.

The ability to hold these two aspects of the cross together is very unusual. There has been a tendency in Christian history either to dwell on the cosmic meaning of the cross or to emphasise a personal and emotional response to the crucified Christ. The hymns of the Church particularly reflect feelings of personal response to the cross. The following is a verse from the well-known hymn, 'O sacred head, once wounded'. It contains very familiar sentiments.

> O Lord of Life and glory
> What bliss till now was Thine!
> I read the wondrous story,
> I joy to call thee mine.
> Thy grief and Thy compassion
> Were all for sinner's gain;
> Mine, mine was the transgression,
> But Thine the deadly pain.

The intensity of that expression sometimes means it is difficult to make sense of the various theological explanations of the atonement. The idea that there is some kind of legal satisfaction demanded by God hardly seems to square with the experience of God as a loving Father.

Some scholars suggest that the story of the prodigal son is a prototype for the resurrection. It contains the themes of death and resurrection – 'this my son who was dead is alive again'. The father is portrayed as willing to accept disgrace in the eyes of his neighbours, so great was his overwhelming love for his erring son. That same love motivated the sending of Jesus to reclaim those who had ignored the heavenly father. Would this kind of loving God insist that Jesus had to be put to death in order to strike some kind of bizarre cosmic bargain with the forces of evil? It is hard for those who have been attracted by divine love to grasp a more abstract cosmic drama.

Many believers have reacted with horror to some of the more seemingly mechanistic presentations of the atonement. Echoing that feeling, some scholars have attempted to explain the significance of the cross purely in terms of the love of God and the moral influence of the cross. In other words, they have wanted to suggest that Christ's example in dying on a cross for a moral cause encourages and inspires others to live differently. The most famous instigator of such an approach was the medieval thinker, Peter Abelard (1079–1142). His words have a curiously modern ring for many: 'How cruel and wicked it seems that anyone should demand the blood of an innocent person as the price for anything, or that it should in any way please him that an innocent man should be slain – still less that God should consider the death of his Son so agreeable that by it he should be reconciled to the whole world!'[1]

These are strong words and Abelard proceeds to explain his view that the cross brings about profound change in those who witness and understand the depth of God's love manifested at Calvary. His thinking was that love begets love and that the potential response will be a profound change of the heart and will be sufficient to produce 'a new form of ethical living of the same basic pattern as that of the Redeemer Himself'.[2] In this sense the love of God is not just manifested to us so much as generated in us.

Unfortunately, Abelard is not very clear as to how this love of God is generated within us and so his thought was open to at least three major criticisms. First, if Abelard is correct then the action of Christ on the cross is limited entirely by human response and nothing objective has taken place in terms of the defeat of evil. While it is true that the benefits of the cross can only be received by the individual when there is an individual response, Christians have always wanted to take very seriously the Scriptures which seem to indicate that a much more objective victory has been won, almost regardless of human response.

Second, Abelard does not take sin and evil seriously enough. In his theory, it is almost as though sin is confined to moral failure while evil is merely the absence of good. Any sense of the active and malevolent power of evil to corrupt at very fundamental levels beyond that of the individual actions of human beings seems to be absent.

Third, it is not at all clear in Abelard's work as to how the death of Christ on a cross does portray the love of God. He is open to exactly the same criticism that he levels against others, namely that this action could just as easily be seen as the cruelty of God as it might be the love of God.

It is perhaps not surprising that Abelard's view never became a dominant position in his own time. However, in the nineteenth century, the German theologian, Friedrich Schleiermacher, attempted to develop Abelard's thought to take account of the criticisms that had been levelled against him. He took the key thoughts of Abelard and placed them in the context of the community of followers of Jesus. Paul Fiddes describes Schleiermacher's thought in this way:

> He is the heir of Abelard in so far as he found the atoning power of Christ's life and death to lie in the transforming of human attitudes to God, but more clearly than Abelard he stresses that the presence of the Redeemer cannot be separated from the community of his followers. Schleiermacher believed that a sense of 'absolute dependence' was a universal characteristic of all human experience, and that this was in fact a consciousness of God who is the 'whence' towards which this dependence leans. While human God-consciousness has become confused and broken, Jesus Christ had perfect God-consciousness, and it is this which he communicates to his disciples.[3]

The great strength and attraction of Schleiermacher's approach lies in his emphasis on the community of believers created by the ability of the Christ to produce this profound sense of God consciousness. Those who are believers recognise this as a description of what the Christian community can be like. Indeed the awareness of God and the different way of looking at the world induced by such a knowledge is clearly an element that has encouraged many to become followers of Jesus. For Schleiermacher the objective element lies in the moral power of being reconciled to God through Christ. It is this new moral relationship that brings a forgiveness of past sin. At an experiential or subjective level, redemption comes through an awareness of the overwhelming love of God. That experience is sufficiently strong to ensure that the power of evil is broken.

However, even apart from some profound issues surrounding Schleiermacher's basic Christology, two key criticisms that were also levelled at Abelard remain. Evil is not taken seriously enough and the objective fact of something having happened at the cross that deals with evil remains weak. It is almost as if the views of people like Abelard and Schleiermacher depend on a kind of optimistic view of humanity's potential which only actually prevails when the dominance of a Christian ethic insulates people to a degree from the awful potential of evil. In a broadly Christian culture, it is all too easy to underestimate the evil of evil.

Those who live at the end of a century centred on the holocaust are more acutely sensitive to the need to see the corrupting and pervasive power of evil. The assumption that love prevails because it is self-evidently superior to hatred and oppression seems impossibly naive to those who stand the other side of ethnic cleansing and the madness of dictators from Stalin to Pol Pot.

Evil and the victory of the God of love

It is no coincidence that the twentieth century was a time when a radical view of the cross emerged to stress the victory of Christ over the cosmic powers of evil. This view, propounded particularly by Gustuv Aulen in his book *Christus Victor*, written some sixty years ago, has become known as the 'classic' view of the atonement. Aulen's view stressed the idea of the dramatic encounter between God and the powers of evil. Colin Gunton quotes Aulen's self-portrayal of his views:

> This type of view may be described provisionally as the 'dramatic'. Its central theme is the idea of the Atonement as a Divine conflict and victory; Christ – Christus Victor – fights against and triumphs over the evil powers of the world, the 'tyrants' under which mankind is in bondage and suffering, and in Him God reconciles the world to Himself.[4]

Aulen summarises it again later in his book:

> God in Christ overcomes the hostile powers which hold man in bondage. At the same time, these hostile powers are also the executants of God's will. The patristic theology is dualistic, but it is not an absolute Dualism. The deliverance of man from the power of death and the devil is at the same time his deliverance from God's judgement. God is reconciled by His own act in reconciling the world to Himself.[5]

Aulen argues that this classic view was developed through Irenaeus, Origen, Athanasius, the Cappadocian Fathers and Augustine, but that the centrality of this theory had been lost because Tertullian and Cyprian had introduced the notion of satisfaction (later developed by Anselm and referred to in the chapter about atonement as sacrifice). Aulen refers to this as the Latin doctrine, which he claims to be legalistic, rationalistic and blind to the central teachings of the Fathers. He sees a sharp contrast between the atonement conceived as a transaction, of a legal kind, and as a drama, in which something decisive happens to change the relations between God and humanity. He strongly stresses that it is a divine victory.

Gunton comments:

> The pattern is clear. Aulen claims that, according to the classic theory the cross of Christ is conceived – metaphorically, we might say – as a divine victory over certain powers of evil which are both evil and within divine control. Reconciliation is achieved because after the Incarnation and death of Christ their power to do harm is taken away by God.[6]

So has the 'classical' theory of the atonement managed to overcome the apparently morally distasteful notion of God demanding a payment, while at the same time recognising the reality of the conflict with evil at a cosmic level and not merely at the level of individual wrongdoing? Has Aulen succeeded in recovering the true doctrine of the early Church Fathers and exposing the errors of the Western Latin, legal theories? Is the attractive theme of drama more helpful than that of legal transaction?

Almost but not quite would seem to be the general verdict. Aulen certainly succeeds in reminding the Christian community about the elements of cosmic conflict which are contained as profound images in Scripture, but there are certainly some problems in Aulen's account of the cross and its effect. Essentially there are three problems.

First, it is difficult to compress all of the biblical material into a dramatic encounter of cosmic proportions. While it is certainly true that the devil was present to tempt Jesus at the beginning of his ministry and that Jesus encounters the powers of evil at various points in his ministry, not least in exorcism, that does not tell the whole story. There is also a very human struggle that sits alongside the cosmic drama. The devil does not feature in the accounts of the struggle that Jesus had in the garden of Gethsemane. He was alone with his personal struggle.

Second, there is a danger in seeing the total drama of the cross entirely through the lens of the victory of Christ. It is possible that the victory becomes the escape from death as compared with that which was accomplished by Christ's actual death on the cross itself. Viewed in such a way, the resurrection represents the moment of victory and the cross only a necessary dramatic counterpoint along the way. But as John Stott rightly points out, the Scripture never says that 'Christ rose for sins' but rather that 'he died for our sins'. The victory over sin cannot simply be ignored in favour of a larger dramatic victory over the powers that stand behind evil, no matter how causal their relationship with sin might be.

Third, in a strange kind of way, the very emphasis on the dramatic encounter with the powers of evil actually underscores the significance of evil. Aulen's very insistence that God has taken away the power of evil to do harm suggests that the important drama is somehow detached from the very human world that we inhabit. The drama is of such cosmic proportions that it hardly seems to connect with human existence and involvement. It seems essential that we embrace the knowledge that evil, although defeated and overthrown at the cross, is still active and effective in the world. To do otherwise is to live in a state of denial which robs us of the victory and the spiritual weapons that Christ's work on the cross has provided us with.

There is a need to integrate the two aspects of the cross. The power of the cross does not lie entirely with the work of God as Aulen wishes to suggest, nor merely in the moral response of men and women. The human and the divine are involved in the event of the cross. Jesus died on the cross as both God and man.

The theologian Walter Wink attempts to bring together both the human and the divine in a drama which is both cosmic and earthly in its scope. He describes how it is possible to disarm the powerful by turning their own aggressive actions against themselves, using non-violent action. He sees 'the powers' as more than the people who run things. They are 'the systems themselves, the institutions and structures that weave society into an intricate fabric of power and relationships'.[7] They are necessary and useful – we could do nothing without them. They are responsible, for example, for the industry that produces cigarettes, despite the fact that smoking causes premature death, but they are also responsible for industries that produce life-enhancing and life-saving facilities and equipment. So the powers do good and evil, they are invisible forces that 'shape the present and dictate the future'.[8]

Wink believes that the powers are spiritual forces that influence in a corporate way as well as in individual lives, and can be understood as representing the corporate personality of, for example, a church. He bases this on Revelation 2 where each of the seven letters are addressed to the congregation's angel, which implies that:

> Every business, corporation, school, denomination, bureaucracy, sports team – indeed, social reality in all its forms – is a combination of both visible and invisible, outer and inner, physical and spiritual. Right at the heart of the most materialistic institutions in society we find spirit . . . which is not always benign. It is just as likely to be pathological. And this is where the biblical understanding of the Powers surpasses in profundity the best of modern sociology. For the angel of an institution is not just the sum total of all that an institution is (which sociology is competent to describe); it is also the bearer of that institution's divine vocation (which sociology is not able to discern). Corporations and governments are 'creatures' whose sole purpose is to serve the general welfare. And when they refuse to do so, their spirituality becomes diseased. They become 'demonic'.[9]

If we are to conquer the demonic influences in our society, we have to recall its angel to its divine task. This may seem to be an overwhelming task in the face of the sheer amount of suffering and brutality that is present in the world throughout the domination system. Wink wondered how, even in the midst of such evil, that the New Testament writers could insist that Christ is sovereign over the powers. He asks, 'And how can we overcome evil without doing evil, and becoming evil ourselves?'[10] How can we respond to violence without resorting to violence ourselves? Wink realised that at one time he did really believe that if all else failed, violence would save, and that meant that no matter how much he might object to any particular form of domination, he was still trusting domination and violence to bring about justice and peace. Somehow he had to discover a way to break the spiral of violence. He found the answer in the power of the cross.

Wink, too, discovered that at the cross, evil turned back on itself. Although the powers mocked Jesus, spat on him, struck him and ridiculed him, 'although they stripped him naked and crucified him in humiliation, this very act also stripped them of the last covering that disguised the towering wrongness of the whole way of living that their violence defended.'[11] The writer of Colossians asserts just this:

And you, who were dead in trespasses and the uncircumcision of your flesh, God made alive together with him, having forgiven us all our trespasses, having cancelled the charge that stood against us with its legal demands; this he set aside, nailing it to the cross. Unmasking the Principalities and Powers, God publicly shamed them, exposing them in Christ's triumphal procession by means of the cross. (Colossians 2:13–15)

What killed Jesus was not irreligion, but religion itself; not lawlessness, but precisely the law; not anarchy, but the upholders of order. It was not the bestial but those considered best who crucified the one in whom the divine Wisdom was visibly incarnate. And because he was not only innocent, but the very embodiment of true religion, true law, and true order, this victim exposed their violence for what it was: not the defence of society, but an attack against God.[12]

Elsewhere Wink demonstrates how we, too, can expose and thus disarm the powers, by embracing Jesus' third way.[13] He suggests that people instinctively respond to violence in one of two ways, by fight or flight. Jesus offers a third way: non-violent direct action (Matthew 5:38–42). This does not mean non-resistance: let the oppressor perpetrate evil unopposed. This interpretation has become a basis for systematic training in cowardice, as Christians are taught to acquiesce to evil. Cowardice is not associated with Jesus.

John Dear in *The God of Peace* argues for a covenant of non-violence which invites us into God's own life of non-violence and grace. The Gospel stories explain that Jesus embodies the covenant of non-violence which invites us to become a people of peace. He believes that the violence that the world suffers today is not a punishment but a natural consequence of our violent actions. To fulfil our side of the covenant we have to renounce all violence, make peace, seek justice for the poor, love our enemies, forgive, etc. Like Wink, he believes that we institutionalise our rejection and set up structures that maintain our brokenness. When we are faithful to the covenant of non-violence, then God will reign on earth.

Ending the cycle of violence

The story is told of a man who had a bad day at work. His employer had unfairly abused him with unfounded accusations and criticism. Not surprisingly, when he arrived home, he carried a good deal of unexpressed anger and potential violence. It didn't take long for that anger to be unfairly visited on his wife. She in turn, having experienced harsh attitudes and words, turned quickly on the eldest child who happened to enter the room at that moment. A stream of invective flowed. The child felt angry and hurt and ran from the room. The child's younger sister was next in line. The same kind of torrent of anger and abuse flowed. The youngest child also felt aggrieved but had no-one else on whom to visit her feelings of pain. She fled instead to her bedroom and picked up a rag doll. The doll was pummelled, kicked and finally thrown against the wall where it lay in a small shapeless pile. Not surprisingly the doll did not fight back. The cycle of anger and violence had finally been absorbed and ended.

In its own small way, the rag doll illustrates one aspect of the action of Christ upon the cross. Like the rag doll, the cycle of violence ended with the death of Christ. Jesus was a willing innocent who chose not to speak in his own defence but to remain entirely silent. But the point of breaking the cycle of violence is not simply to allow violence to pass by without comment. It is also to allow new beginnings and new stories to emerge which are fundamentally different in their structure.

It is at this point that it is right and indeed essential to view the cross in the context of both the incarnation and the resurrection. By entering our world in the incarnation, God first declared himself interested in the plight of all victims – the poor, the oppressed and the weak. God is fundamentally concerned with justice. The cross is important in absorbing the wrong that has been done but without the resurrection it does not necessarily suggest a new future. Hope begins on the cross by offering an end to previous cycles of recrimination and blame but the resurrection offers a startling declaration of hope for the future.

The writings of our sisters and brothers from African, Asian and South American contexts demonstrates how essential that connection is. The cross emphasises that the struggle for a new way of being is never without pain and suffering. Martyrdom and sacrifice are part of

God's new way and must never be devalued as only a cosmic drama. As Yacob Tesfai declares:

> The cross is the road that leads to the resurrection, and the resurrection has no meaning without the cross. 'The cross is the historical meaning of the resurrection . . . This means that the resurrection should not be separated from the cross . . . Once it becomes separated from the cross, the resurrection separates itself from history.' The cross must also be viewed in the light of the resurrection. Viewed so, it transcends itself and creates hope in the future born through its birthpangs . . . In this way, the resurrection has the power to kindle hope even in the midst of the most meaningless crosses.[14]

Perhaps the most powerful practical demonstration of that connectivity can be seen in the attempts of the new South Africa to forge a beginning that is dramatically different from the outcome that many expected. The insistence that forgiveness must flow from a proper confession of previous crimes reveals a conviction that truth is an important ingredient in facing a new future. The determination to offer forgiveness rather than insist on rigorous recrimination represents an attempt, no matter how incomplete, to build a future that includes both a recognition of the pain of the struggle and a new hope for tomorrow. Few can deny that the Christian experience of the cross and the resurrection have shaped this astonishing development.

Questions

1. Do you feel that God is presented by Christians as somehow unjust in demanding that the death of Jesus is necessary in the fight against evil?

2. Do politicians or social commentators really take seriously enough the evil of evil?
3. How do you respond to the accusation of many critics of Christianity that religion is the cause of much violence and evil?
4. What do you think of the idea that evil can be embodied in institutions as much as in individuals?
5. Do you think that the resurrection is more important as a message of hope than the crucifixion?

Notes

1. John Stott, *The Cross of Christ*, Inter-Varsity Press, Leicester, 1986, p.217.
2. F.W. Dillistone, *The Christian Understanding of Atonement*, SCM Press Ltd, London, 1968/94, p.325.
3. Paul Fiddes, *Past Event and Present Salvation*, Darton, Longman & Todd, London, 1989, p.161.
4. Colin Gunton, *The Actuality of Atonement*, T & T Clark Ltd, Edinburgh, 1988, p.4.
5. *Ibid.*, p.59.
6. *Ibid.*, p.55.
7. Walter Wink, *The Powers That Be*, Doubleday, New York, 1998, p.1.
8. *Ibid.*, p.3.
9. *Ibid.*, pp.4–5.
10. *Ibid.*, p.7.
11. *Ibid.*, p.83.
12. Walter Wink, *Engaging the Powers*, Fortress Press, Minneapolis, 1992, pp.139–140.
13. *Ibid.*, p.175f.
14. Yacob Tesfai, *The Scandal of a Crucified World*, p.49f.

8

The Cross and our Present Cry

This final chapter attempts to find ways in which we might speak about the cross in our present time. It explores the way in which the cross offers contemporary people direction, meaning and hope. In closing, it attempts to relate the meaning of the cross to the whole of Christian life.

The Cross and our Present Cry

So far in this book, we have surveyed the many ways in which the greatest writers and thinkers have spoken about the cross over the centuries. But how can we speak about the cross in this new century? It should be apparent from all that we have already explored that the cross is such a vast drama that we need to approach it from a number of perspectives in order to gain any kind of meaningful understanding of what the cross really signifies. David Ford, Regius Professor of Divinity at Cambridge writes of the cross:

> These interconnected, very early elements of a story and two rituals are at the centre of an array of imagery with which early and later Christians tried to do justice to the event, which they found incomparably mysterious, moving, and significant.
>
> It is as if the range of significance of the crucifixion was to be indicated by drawing on every sphere of reality to represent it.[1]

While it is undoubtedly true that we need to think of the cross by using every metaphor and theory, it is likely that some are more helpful than others for this present age. This is not to say that our own times are unique in this respect. It is clear that the anxieties and concerns of every age hugely impact the way in which believers have approached the cross. For example, in the Victorian age, which experienced a curious combination of hope about the future with a high incidence of infant mortality, interest and concern about the next life, heaven and how one might gain assurance of access to paradise, was an understandable and widespread concern.

Other ages, such as the seventeenth century, have arguably been more concerned with a desire to please God in this life and so have been acutely aware of what we might call the seriousness of sin and so of human guilt before God. The medieval period had a particular interest in honour, duty and exercising good deeds. All of these core concerns naturally influenced the way in which the Christian community tended to think about the efficacy and importance of the cross.

What then are the anxieties or concerns that occupy the attention of our contemporary Western society? There are a number of connected themes that many social commentators have noted as core concerns for late twentieth-century Western culture. The reality of war and holocaust has left its own profound impressions. For the first time since the campaigns of Ghengis Khan, civil populations in Western Europe have found themselves as involved in warfare as the armies which have been in conflict. Even when our own civilian population has not been drawn into a particular conflict, television footage has brought an awareness of death and destruction which has moved war a long way from any romantic notions of heroism and bravery.

This reality of the seemingly inevitable incidence of war – man's inhumanity to man on a colossal scale – has coincided with deep doubts about an earlier myth – the inevitability of progress. Science and technology have been seen to have their own moral and practical limits as compared with an earlier mythic belief in their omnipotence, and even infallibility. Deep doubt about the direction of science has become attached to an awareness that for the first time in human history we have the capacity to end all human life rather than to have life ended by the apparently random and capricious forces of nature.

If this is true at a macro level in our culture, then there has been no easy escape in a compensatory human solidarity. The stories which have sustained cultural life, especially the Judao-Christian story, have been abandoned while meaningful community has been undermined by the advance of a radical individualism which seems to have called into doubt the notion of any kind of community, even that as basic as the nuclear human family.

The maelstrom produced by the combination of the loosening of cultural connectivity with a past story and uncertainty about whether any cohesive story might take its place has led to a widespread conviction that life has no meaning whatsoever. Any meaning which we might construct for our own life is not part of a wider structure. It merely derives from our own experiences, views and preferences, in short, what 'works' for us and possibly our immediate circle of contacts. The core anxiety surrounding the issue of the meaninglessness of life represents a concern that does not connect easily with traditional understandings of the cross and its purpose. Certainly, the various satisfaction or legal theories about the purpose of the cross which might well have addressed the concerns of a different age in relation to an awareness of human sin and guilt have a distinctly hollow ring if used to explore the problem of a lack of meaning in life itself.

Beyond this difficulty lie two more problems. First, the age in which we live is in the midst of profound and rapid change. It is possible that we may come through this time of change and emerge again with a new set of confident boundaries which may guide us to a more certain cultural climate. We cannot yet know whether this will happen or if it did what approaches to the cross would be appropriate in such a new situation. We therefore need responses which can live with the transitional nature of our present times. Second, there is little disagreement that consumerism represents a dominant theme at the level of popular culture. There is a huge conflict of opinion within the Christian community as to how the Christian message, and in particular the message of the cross, should be presented in relation to this contemporary phenomenon. In very general terms, one response is to look to the cross as something which is entirely opposed to the spirit of consumerism and which therefore speaks in judgement on our age. The other extreme is to seek to package Christianity as a product which competes effectively in the marketplace for attention alongside every other product. If we are to take the first view then in one sense we do not need to worry about interpreting the cross for our present age. It only has to be proclaimed as prophetic judgement. The second response does require effective packaging but how do you attractively wrap an event which is both scandal and folly? Clearly it would be all too easy to ignore the redemptive power of the cross in favour of a presentation which sees the cross only in terms of its palliative impact. In short, the cross becomes a better therapy for our individual needs as compared with other available therapies. The cross can never be reduced to such a gift-wrapped accessory status. But equally it is not true to say that we should not speak of the genuine blessing of the cross for our daily existence.

So what can we say about the cross in the midst of the cry of this age for direction, meaning and hope especially in the context of the drive to consume at any cost? I want to suggest that the particular problems of our times require a combination of three very different approaches. First, it is essential to find ways to speak of a cosmic drama. We need to know that the universe makes sense because ultimately we can never derive meaning from the starting point of our own experience. We live against a broader canvas that requires interpretation.

Second, it must be possible to connect personal encounters with that broader picture. It can never be enough to ask people to subdue their personal feelings in an act of the will simply to believe that because the universe is secure so are we. Our personal world needs to connect with that wider truth in meaningful ways. In emphasising the personal story of individuals, we may find that we do not begin with the cross so much as with the incarnation. God first demonstrated his love for us by seeking to be one with us. A declaration of the amazing and embracing love of God is possibly the most potent motif for helping people to explore a God encounter in our present age. It is not that we stop with the incarnation because the incarnation leads naturally to the redemptive reality of the cross. But we may have to begin with God's identification with us if we are ever to present the demands that the cross makes on us for profound change.

Third, the experience of the Church needs to demonstrate

the validity of the message. It can never be enough for the Church to be a collection of individual stories which connect with a wider cosmic story. Somehow the reality of that story needs to become clear in the way in which the Church shares its life together and with the wider world. In talking about that collective life, we cannot avoid talk of the cross as a redemptive act. The point about redemption is not merely that God has done something for us so much as the fact that he calls us to live changed lives. We are redeemed from something and for something. The story of the cross is not complete without talk of the way of the cross. In the New Testament we are called to be witnesses. It is no coincidence that the word for witness later became our English word for martyr. The way of the cross is a call to a cause, namely the working out on earth of the realities of the kingdom. Through the cross we are sustained by the life of God which brings the quality of the eternal into the present fragmentary experience that we live each day.

None of these approaches can ever be enough by themselves but, taken together, we will be able to speak sensitively to an aching world.

The God who suffers

St Paul saw very clearly that the cross represented a 'scandal to Jews' and a 'stumbling block to the Greeks'. The idea that the God who stands behind the universe, an omnipotent, all powerful God, could suffer and die in ignominy by public execution always carries the potential to shock and dismay religious people. This is not how we like to think of God. At first glance it is far from comfortable. The cross is as shocking today for Muslims as it was for Jews in the time of Paul.

In the same way the cross as a solution to evil seems strange to those who are intellectuals confident of their own solutions to the profound problems of evil and human suffering. For such as these the cross is still a stumbling block – incomprehensible religious jargon. However, I want to suggest that in our time the brash confidence of an earlier secularism has been found wanting in the face of the horror of the holocaust and many other tragedies. There is a profound irony in the fact that for centuries, secularism has rightly pointed the finger at the capacity of religion to feed a hunger for conflict and war and now, in the very century of secular influence, wars in Europe and elsewhere have been more brutal, more devastating, and have killed greater numbers than ever before. It is clear that war as a manifestation of evil and suffering is not primarily a religious problem but a human one.

Among the more thoughtful this awareness induces a degree of humility and searching. In such a climate the notion of the God who comes and suffers with us and for us ceases to be a stumbling block. Instead, it represents a point of hope. To quote Cardinal Basil Hume:

> If I look long enough at the figure of Christ dying on the cross I begin to see that his passion and death had a purpose which is directly related to our own suffering. For the suffering that Jesus endured provides consolation and guidance in our greatest pain. As we look at the cross we should venerate it and embrace it in our prayer. It will slowly give up its secret, not suddenly but over the years and Christ's suffering will lead us to new life.[2]

The image of the God who suffers with us does not represent a doctrine of the atonement, and the various theories that come to us down the centuries have their part to play in later contemplation of the mystery of the cross. But mysteries have to be apprehended before they can ever be comprehended, no matter how partially. That apprehension begins with the declaration that the one who died on the cross was not just another criminal but God himself. It is this declaration above all others that makes the death of Jesus the most famous death in history. As one author puts it: 'No mere man; no third party, no angel, but God himself was present in a unique way in the person and the sufferings of Jesus on Calvary . . . That is what makes the cross so special: the identity of the sufferer. There never has been and never will be a parallel to that.'[3]

The unveiling of the character of God that is seen in the apparent humiliation of God in giving himself up, silently and meekly to execution, goes to the very heart of the nature of the universe. It speaks of ultimate power. It conveys in stark reality that when all is said and done there are only two powers in cosmic conflict. One is the love of power, the other is the power of love. These two forces met on the cross and ultimately we are drawn to choose one of these powers with which to align our lives and our future.

Because we meet these realities in our existential encounter with life, our apprehension of this cosmic drama may need to be more mystical than conceptual in nature. (It is worth noting in passing that even in the world of science there has come a tendency towards awe and wonder as a consequence of increased knowledge.) The mystics of the ages help us to understand these feelings. The medieval mystic Julian of Norwich pointed to her awareness of the structure of the universe as an embrace of divine love. The words with which she is most associated – 'All will be well, and all manner of things shall be well' – is not a statement of disconnected naivety, a woolly optimism. Rather she sought to convey that in her struggle with pain and the coming possibility of death she had met with God and discovered that in the finality of all things, the love of God is the ultimate reality, the final destination of the universe. That love is powerfully present in the actual death of God on a cross, helpless, yet undefeated, weak and broken, yet able to overcome hell itself.

Encounters with the cross

The mystical revelations of Julian of Norwich are echoed in the very ordinary encounters of everyday believers. The following three accounts are the stories of three believers known to me. I have selected these three precisely because they are not the famous and the exceptional but the known and the fallible.

The story of Rick Lewis

In many ways, Rick Lewis' journey to faith could be seen as the kind of path that would have been much more common when churches could normally expect the children of church members to automatically become Christians. Such a pattern is hardly the norm today. As the previous sentence suggests, Rick grew up in a church family and attended his local church regularly with his family. For most of his early years church was a good place to be, somewhere where he had made friends and enjoyed attending. But beyond the social and family meaning, the message of Christianity made no special impact until, around the age of ten, he joined a Sunday school class which had more challenge to it. Partly because of the influence of this new class he began attending Sunday evening services where the gospel message was more obviously and intentionally preached. Even here though there seemed to be more emphasis on the importance of belonging to the church than on any specific biblical content.

However, on one occasion, Rick was impacted by a particular gospel message. It was a sermon on the cross and its meaning. The one element that communicated to Rick as a young person was the simple message that Christ had died on the cross, not just for everyone, true as that might be, but also for Rick Lewis. Following the sermon there came an appeal for people who wished to commit their lives to Christ to come forward and Rick did so with some confusion, shaking, in the midst of an intense experience that he couldn't necessarily understand at that time. It was what he called 'a God encounter at a heart level but not a head level'.

In keeping with the tradition of which he was a part, Rick was 'followed up' and then baptised by total immersion. The experience still didn't make much sense beyond a feeling that Jesus loved him and that he had made a response to an overwhelming apprehension of the love of God. It took some years in his mid-teens before he began to unpack and understand what had happened. Once again, the process of understanding took place in the context of a good mid-teens group, in particular through the influence of a leader who taught him about the faith and to play the guitar.

His subsequent involvement in missions with the inevitable opposition to his faith caused him to think more deeply about his beliefs and experience and this process continued during his studies at Bible college. For Rick, his early response to the cross and his later understanding of what it meant has produced a sense of being on a life journey. The themes of love, suffering and sacrifice, flowing intensely from the drama of the cross have provided long-term sustaining themes through which to interpret that same life journey.

The story of Pete Bowen

Unlike Rick Lewis, Pete Bowen was not brought up in a family that regularly attended church. As a young child, around seven or eight years old, Pete was sent to Sunday school but did not attend church with his parents. His experience of Sunday school was short lived and little penetrated his memory from that time. Later he attended a church-related youth group which meant occasional visits to family services. While he remembers some Bible stories and passages from religious education at school, Pete's exposure to Christianity had no personal application and ended completely around the age of fifteen.

By the time Pete was in his late teens and early twenties, he was exploring many ideas and ideologies. This was the early 1970s and Pete joined a commune where the members were experimenting with a variety of alternative lifestyles. Pete does not remember an active search for God but some secular pop songs raised a number of questions about meaning. He remembers the words of a Black Sabbath song as 'I need someone to show me the things in life that I can't find'. A Pink Floyd song also had an impact:

Ticking away the moments that make up a dull day
You fritter and waste the hours in an offhand way

Kicking around on a piece of ground in your hometown
Waiting for someone or something to show you the way.

These words and others had something of a subliminal
influence. However, the search for meaning was not nearly
as important as party life, alcohol and drugs.

During the commune experience, Pete became involved
in a number of occult practices and while under the influence of LSD attempted astral projection. In ways that he
finds difficult to explain and even describe, Pete had what
he calls a God encounter while engaged in astral projection. That encounter pointed him to the Christ. He had a
deep sense that Christ was in some way the answer. Alongside that feeling came a deep awareness of being loved and
that at the heart of reality was someone rather than no-one
or nothing. During his experience a voice came from deep
within which seemed to ask the question, 'Who is your
Saviour?' His response in that moment was to reply, 'Jesus
Christ.'

In some ways this encounter was both affirming and
frightening and Pete searched out a local church that one
of his commune friends had recently begun to attend. In
that context he began to put together what he calls 'a
jigsaw of evidence'. A reasoned explanation of that which
he had encountered helped him to interpret his experience.
During that exploration he came to see the cross as the
focal point which explained how it was that Christ was his
Saviour. It was for him the heart of God's action to
express his love for the world in general and for Pete in
a personal sense. Today he would say that the cross represents hope – hope of the reality of forgiveness, hope that
he can be reconciled with God and with others. It remains
a central theme for his ongoing relationship with God.

Mary Publicover's story

Mary's story contrasts with both Pete's and Rick's story in
that she remembers a deep sense of the love of God and
meaningful times of prayer before she came to a moment
of significant encounter with God. Mary was brought up
in a Christian family all of whom attended church and she
was educated in a church school. In her mid-teens she was
aware that some of her friends were actively choosing
against God and religion whereas she had positive feelings
towards both. The sense of inclining towards God formed
a backdrop for an organised year retreat which was
arranged by the church school. The whole school year
were obliged to attend a Jesuit retreat held in a retreat
centre. Mary was sixteen at the time and this three-day
silent retreat was something that she willingly embraced
and yet which held unexpected depth.

Mary sensed that the priest who led the retreat had a
passionate love for God and was someone who conveyed a
feeling of vulnerability. The event meant enough that she
can still remember the name of the priest and the feelings
associated with the surroundings, the garden and the trees,
one particular tree with branches that reached down to the
ground and formed a kind of seat, even the smell of polish
– that ubiquitous prompter of memories.

Although the retreat was silent for the participants, it
included some teaching sessions which covered subjects
such as prayer, forgiveness and the love of God. Naturally
the themes of forgiveness and love centred on the death of
Jesus on the cross. That teaching helped Mary to see for
the first time the relationship between her awareness of the
love of God, and so of his forgiveness, with the death of
Jesus. The retreat included an opportunity to come

forward and make a personal confession. In such a context this was not merely a matter of religious ritual or duty but a deeply personal response. For Mary this was a very specific time of being aware of the love of God and of falling in love with Jesus because of his forgiving action on the cross.

Some decades later, the cross is important to Mary as a dynamic and potent symbol guaranteeing the love of God. She sees the cross as indicating the broader redemptive activity of God. God always seeks to work through weakness to restore and redeem communities of people as well as individuals so that life can be infused with hope.

Creating community

For all three of these individuals the cross represents a powerful motif which allows an integration of meaning in the cosmos with personal existence. The love of God makes sense of life. The cross is the point at which the love of God touches the created order and connects with the culmination of all things. The personal experiential encounter with God combined with a growing awareness that we are connected to a deeper reality in the cosmos is privately powerful. But for redemption to be meaningful in terms of the kingdom of God, the very kingdom announced by Jesus and mysteriously birthed by the cross, the private has also to become very public.

The Church is called to live as a prophetic community demonstrating the grace of God as publicly as possible. It is in the heat of the crucible of the Church that forgiveness is tested in the creation of relationships and the painful forge of forgiveness. What is shaped on such an anvil can become a place of hope and health for all. It is in the place of genuine community that the true importance of the cross can be known.

The danger of this book and indeed of most books on the cross, lies precisely in the attempt to understand the cross by dissecting its meaning too intensely. The very separation of the work of the cross into atonement theories, the parting of this event from all the other events in the life of Jesus can actually undo the meaning of the cross as much as illumine it. It is our attempt to live out the message of the cross as a community of followers of Jesus that brings a coherence and unity to the event of the death of Jesus. To attempt to live as a community of the incarnation, the cross and the resurrection merely as an expression of true life communicates the heart of the cross in a way that mere analysis never can. It is therefore essential that we see the power of the love of God manifesting itself in and through the Church.

Of all the churches in all the world I would like to describe just one church, not because it is the only grace-filled congregation nor even the best but simply as a concrete reminder of what the Church is called to manifest. The church in question is called the South Melbourne Restoration Community and is based in the urban setting of inner-city Melbourne. The area has become somewhat gentrified in recent years. Many older residents who have lived there for many years are also part of the community. Some who might be described as poor working class people live in the area. South Melbourne is also well known as a centre for the gay and lesbian community. A good number of artistic bohemians live in this neighbourhood. It also contains the red light community. This unusual mixture is not always fertile territory for church life.

One particular church in the neighbourhood began more than 100 years ago and up until ten years ago was not thriving. Around that time there came a significant renewal following the arrival of a new leadership team. The team was led by Alan Hirsch, his wife Debra and a second couple, John and Sharon Patriki. Their initial intention was not so much to conduct evangelism as to construct a community experience for those on the edges of society. People started to come because they were hungry for community. The church was soon composed of misfits and 'human debris' to quote Alan Hirsch.

A good number of the early community members had come from the gay and lesbian community which gave a particular nuance of acceptance as a theme in the emerging new church. Former prostitutes joined the church as did a mixture of 'street people' many of whom had used drugs and alcohol. A sense of God's love and acceptance pervaded the development of what became a place where people knew how to have fun, to be real, where they attempted to serve God, and were concerned to accept people exactly as they were. In short, it was a community of grace with a strong awareness of the centrality of Christ as one who had also hung around with the broken and the needy.

Those who came knew they were sinners. There was no need to preach repentance so much as to help people discover how to work out the implications of grace in their lives. The atmosphere that developed could be described as both electric and highly creative. In time a church plant called Matthew's Party was developed with a particular focus on 'street people'. At the moment 90 per cent of the congregation are between the ages of twenty-five and thirty-five so that the church has a strong generation X feel.

How then does the cross figure in the midst of such a church community? At first sight, what matters more than the crucified Christ is an identification with the Jesus who lived among the poor and the outcast, those on the fringes of society. Yet in talking with the leaders of this congregation it soon becomes clear that they have an intuitive sense that an identification with the powerless and the broken is costly, so costly that it feels existentially like the road to Calvary. More than this, it is the power of a love that is willing to lay down its life that ultimately produces the social glue that produces real community in those who have sought to belong elsewhere and have not found a real home. Those who come to seek community also find hope and healing, power to escape multiple addictions in order to live creative lives in freedom. The radical Jesus who lived for outcasts cannot be separated from the crucified and risen Christ. It is Christ in his entirety that produces the vital heartbeat that pumps the energy of this church.

Wherever the Church is found, it is called to exhibit this kind of grace. Not just an acceptance of those who are joining a privileged or select group and who are therefore in some way like those who already belong. It is not a kind of narrow grace defined by doctrinal formula. It is instead a generous, overwhelming, surprising, and fundamentally redeeming grace that flows spontaneously from the heart of a God who describes himself as a Father who cannot help loving. Grace of this order cannot be formed into tidy sentences but rather cries out for people to plunge into it. It is a grace that calls us to be our true selves. It is the inexplicable offer of a God who has poured out himself to such an extent that a place of shame and execution is presented as a living symbol of the greatest healing and hope that the universe has ever witnessed.

As those who are called to live out grace we need always to remember that as those who seek to follow Christ we are also always thirsty for grace. The knowledge that we too are hungry points us to the words of Jesus, 'Blessed are the poor in Spirit.' We might render it, blessed are those who know their need, who acknowledge their thirst. In the spirit of that humility, I close with part of a prayer written by David Adam:

> We come with all your broken people.
> We come with the broken in spirit,
> with the despondent and the despairing.
> We come with the broken in mind,
> with the deeply distressed and the disturbed.
> We come with the broken in body,
> with all who are injured and all who are ill.
> We come to you with all our needs.
> Lord, broken on the cross, we come to you.
> Only you can make us whole.[4]

Questions

1. Can the cross have any meaning in a society where people do not seem to see the need for any kind of salvation or forgiveness from God?
2. Is there a danger that we might present the cross as merely another consumer product with perceived benefits for our well-being?
3. Can you describe an experience you might have had with the event of Christ on the cross? What meaning does the event of Christ dying on a cross have for you?
4. What examples can you think of where forgiveness has been a powerful factor in enabling individuals or a whole group of people to have a new beginning?

5. What does the grace of God (the undeserved love of God) mean for you?

Notes

1. David Ford, *Theology – A Very Short Introduction*, Oxford University Press, 1999, p.120.
2. Basil Hume, *The Mystery of the Cross*, Darton, Longman & Todd, London, 1988, p.97f.
3. Michael Green, *The Empty Cross of Jesus*, Hodder & Stoughton, 1984/95, p.29.
4. David Adam, *Clouds and Glory*, SPCK, UK, 1998, p.57.